Loch Raven Review

Five

Sykesville · Baltimore

Jim Doss   Christopher T. George   Dan Cuddy

Editors

Loch Raven Press

LOCH RAVEN REVIEW, Five

© 2010 by Loch Raven Review

ISSN 1559-6494

Loch Raven Review, published online four times a year and in print once a year, is an international online and print magazine of poetry, translations, fiction, criticism, interviews, and art. *Loch Raven Review* is an independent magazine unaffiliated with any institution. Correspondence, contributions, and submissions are welcome at submissions@lochravenreview.net.

On the cover: Gabriele Münter, *Black Mask With Rose*, 1912, Oil on canvas.

Loch Raven Review

Five

Jim Doss, Editor
Christopher T. George, Editor
Dan Cuddy, Editor

Sykesville · Baltimore

Table of Contents

POETRY

TRANSLATIONS

INTERVIEWS

FICTION

NON-FICTION

ESSAYS

BOOK REVIEWS

Poetry

Coaxing Blossoms

A hummingbird,
bright red at the throat,
dances with the sunflowers
in my son's garden. He is
his mother's boy, born
with his wrists buried
in the ground, coaxing
blossoms from spring storms.
I can not love him more
than I do now.
The way he stares at me
when we talk. Every word drops
into him like rain into rivers.

Sometimes he dances
in the living room.
There is no music,
he just moves his body. He hums
himself a simple rhythm.

the birds

the birds are trying to tell us
was all I heard
avoided and walked past the man
            who told me

pointed to the river as he spoke—
water out with the tide
flat and glacial

only geese and gulls
disturbed its surface
washed wings
paddled about
an occasional arrival and departure

you wanted to ask him what
they were trying to tell us
whether he was aware of
something we all needed to know
a foreboding
a prophecy

but you never did

Preserving

Standing in the kitchen, my mother
prepares to make strawberry jam with
the berries we picked that morning,
our flats filled to the brim.
I carry them inside carefully,
set them on the counter, and wait.
She must notice I've been waiting
to tell her. I begin: "Mother,"
but she is cleaning berries, carefully
dropping a handful in the sink and washing with
cold water. My head lowers, eyes brimming,
alone in quiet mourning.
I want to tell her about that morning
when, still in shock from sheets, his weight,
I watched sunlight fall on the brim
of a cup filled with coffee, set carefully
on a nightstand. What to tell to a mother
who had raised her children with
rosaries, pressing our communion clothes carefully
every Sunday morning?

We pull berries from the water with
a strainer, placing them on a towel, waiting
for the droplets to dry. My mother
pours sugar and pectin over the brim
of a large pan that's soon brimming
with boiling fruit. We watch it carefully.
She learned the recipe from her mother.

They, too, would spend a summer morning
picking berries in a field, the weight
of the flats measured with
an old scale. Now I watch the pan with
her and wonder if she was ever brimming
to tell someone she hadn't waited
or if she had, instead, carefully
bent down and picked strawberries all morning
in silence, for the sake of her Mother.

Mother asks me if I'm finished with
the jars. I only nod, pressing a lid on every brim.

Some things are worth preserving. I wait.

$7.35

When grandpa died
Goodwill took the Westerns
and videos on Yellowstone.
I took a backpack. The church got
shirts, belts, and the books on Lewis
and Clark and the Victorian Railroads.
Dad, pressed, took the snowshoes.
Cousin Ross took the Deer Antlers
back to his apartment in Idaho.
Cousin Jerry chose a green army coat.
(Later, he pulled out the pockets and found
tissues full of nosebleed).

Grandma scooped the change up
off the top of his dresser, and put the coins
in two plastic bags. The next time my Aunt
drove her into town for milk and the mail,
the last stop they made was the bank.

My grandma told the teller she didn't need
a slip. They drove home, her quietly holding
sixty four years wages in her lap.

Predicament

I feel exactly like a young mother
who buys a book—a biography of Marie
Antoinette and then cannot
push past the opening chapters,
the overbearing Queen, summer retreat,
line of carriages slowly winding
through the forest, the necessary
rouge, everyone watching, nothing
happening, gambling experts brought
in from Paris, the earnest insistence
that one has not been riding horseback.
I feel exactly like a young mother
who bought a book about a young
Austrian girl but is actually only

a new mother, not young, pushing
my cart through the bread aisle,
rolls and loaves lined up
wondering about scarcity,
the anger rising up in the countryside
when the nobles go plowing through
fields as they hunt, thoughtlessly stomping
down the corn, the peasants at this point
still raising a hand in respectful greeting,
but the smile, the bright and fixed smile,
fading away so much more quickly now.

Fannie Kisses Wu Chen

For twenty years I've carried Hung's photo
from flat to flat, placing it
carefully atop the fireplace

affectionately, cautiously
as if it were a thousand year old
Chinese family heirloom.

For weeks Wu Chen has taken me to restaurants.
We talk of Hong Kong,
of how we miss the breakfasts
of congee and deep-fried devils
sold by hawkers.

"My pregnant daughter is embarrassed,"
I confess, "by my advice.
She just rolls her eyes."

Wu Chen nods. "We expect our children
to be like kittens
left at our doorstep," he says. "Grateful. But
they have their own stubborn lives."

In my apartment Wu Chen
tries to kiss me for the first time. I hesitate.
"What is wrong?" he asks.
I sense my deceased husband's disapproval.

I drop my scarf over Hung's picture
and turn back to Wu Chen.

That is when

we kiss.

Your Mother

It didn't matter
if you valued a corner of a sofa
and a nap more than your homework.

Or if your room had more grungy friends
listening to music than a mosh pit.

She cooked your meals even as you grumbled
that the soups were too hot.

She held cool rags to your forehead,
sponged your cheeks as you sighed
and wheezed like a grounded steamer.

Often when you were broke
she left money
in the dirty pockets of your unwashed jeans,
and waited for you to discover your good luck.

She was there to offer you your old room
as you were thrown out of apartments
by landlords with hearts as small as nickels.

She believed you were one job away
from success. Yet you continued to lose jobs
the way you lost quarters at arcades.

When she said you should go back to college
you said she was unreasonable.

You were right. She always

was.

Aunt Viola

She paid five bucks a month to have a star
named after her.
She would point to the sky's crush of stars
and say there it is.

This is the same Viola whose creditors
took away her furniture every quarter
as if her house were a stage set.

Viola, who used to pay me
to pull Spanish moss from her oaks

as she lay in a lounge chair,
the bachelors in the apartment complex
eyeing her through binoculars.

Viola, whose husband came home one night
and threw her lover naked
into the street.
Viola,
who reprimanded her husband
for not trusting her, demanding an apology.

Viola, who I learned today
died several years ago. Viola,
who I suddenly miss. I squint up
at the night sky. I wonder how many times, Viola,

your star has been renamed? It's missing,
as if you didn't keep up the payments.

Like you, reclaimed by your creditors.

10 and 5

I am not a mother yet; I've lost a mother,
but I am not a mother, except to myself
on days I hold my waist and rock, tending
to the weak.

But tomorrow, you (10) and you (5)
will come to visit your father
and I will turn into "the girlfriend." At first
you will dismiss me like a fish swimming
beneath the ice you stand upon.

But what you don't know is one day
I will be your step-mother, the Mama bear
who tucks you in every other week.
I will be there for breakfasts and dinners.
I will want to hear about your day.

Will you (10) let me into your scalded heart?

Will you (5) stop kicking and spitting your pain
enough to see my lap is warm and safe?
Will you be still enough for me to
kiss your head?

And you (10), will you feel trusting enough to tell
me about your first crush and if you do, I'll bring
out that old box of Valentines candy given to me
at age 9. I'll show you the red, shiny heart—
shaped box and we can both giggle.

And when you (10 and 5) go home, your Daddy
and I will smile and I'll no longer need to rock myself...

we watch our kids bound away in the grass
until one week later when we are your
(10 and 5) favorite parents.

The Mother Who Wasn't

Childless, I hold scores of children
inside. I bleed an extra blood-letting
due to confused hormones and I wonder
if I lose them in each clot, these eggs
that go untouched, unfertilized.

Red brings me down.

I remember Mother telling me at twelve
that I bleed to bear babies and I imagined
baby after baby slipping from my uterus
as I fainted on a starch-white bed,
a slide of scarlet leaving me.

Now, with husband and step-children,
I am busy with dishes and homework
and reading bedtime books.
But I still lie in bed; the moon's pull
reaches me through the East window.
The moon wants babies, calls for the
ocean's current to rock me toward birth,
but I continue to let the blood flow each month.

Must I endure this bittersweet sacrifice?
What—who lives inside of me? I cannot
swallow my step-children and make them mine.
I taste a dot of blood and thus
my parallel universe: my babies
crying their vowels to me, my babies who
don't hear their mother missing them so.

Plane crash

Rains mist a gray day
and vapors seep
from dark worlds
within.

They breathe thin ghosts
from nether places,
their chaotic dins dulled
by hard strokes of rain
beating swollen streets to submission.

The lightest breath of burnt things
heats the air.
Life flows on, unaware
of shadows, gathering,
waiting there.

Detour

surely that threadbare tire finally will blow if only
because you're tardy getting to your daughter's school.
A detour to the garage will get you a new tire
installed in less than an hour for $65 however

what if you pulled into this tiny drive, walled in by this
black rubber mountain, in shaky hand its painted sign:
Reyes Tires. This part of town is safe in daylight, right?

he's small and Spanish-speaking but with an accent
not South Texas. His smile says you're not from this
neighborhood, are you? Plucks a tire from the mountain, worn
but not threadbare and rolls it to you: "This is good one."

fifteen dollars, he says, fifteen minutes. Whirs lug nuts off,
kicks the tire to jar it from the wheel, and in ten is done

but who knows who's more embarrassed when he says
"No credit cards." Who knows if he believes you when
you promise to return with cash, and quickly he nods yes

when you lay the bills in the small man's hand,
his smile says he lost a bet with himself. "Thank
you," you say, leaning in, making eye contact.
"Any time."

Morning love poem

the morning lamplight reveals the wife I married,
at her best in the still house, rousing the kids

with a grace that's startling, all crisp movements
and calm intonations, imparting a proficiency
she didn't have the night before

confronted with sluggish children and uncooperative
adults she welcomes the morning's demands

her hands seem to enlarge as she pulls the household
together, decorating us with the rudiments of morning:

food and clothing, soap and toothpaste

operating with the quiet gratitude
of an old physician doing God's work

as if she were created for this stage
I was walking my dog in the park one day
when something scampered in front of me
and I nearly tripped. As it floated away I saw
it was the words *he likes her 4 a friend.* ;-)

I thought it odd.

But before I could ponder it more, I
noticed another one snaking around
the edge of a jungle gym: *Who's going
to pay for mother's care?* It slithered
around a swing set and disappeared.

It was then that I looked around and saw
words floating everywhere, high and low,
over picnic tables, through a basketball hoop
and between spokes of kids' bikes as they
rode on the sidewalk. *what kind of hamburger
helper do u want?* one string said.

I saw an *OMG* caught in a cottonwood,
until it wriggled loose. Two *LOLs* were
tangled on a slide, straining to break free.

I WAS SHITFACED,
one chain proclaimed and
scooted off into the distance. I noticed several *wuz up????s.*
Others were declarative: *I'm in line at DMV*
and *The mayor's tie has polar bears on it.*

Feeling a little uncomfortable, I started walking
toward my car, when my eyes fixed on a chunk
of conversation sliding across the hood. I felt like an
eavesdropper. *it's YOURS. if you didn't want this
you should have brought a condom. MAN UP.*

I think I may have blushed a little.

I knew it was time to go home when one whipped

by me from behind, grazing my ear. *I'm your niece,*
for Christ's sake! Your flesh and blood. How could
you do this to me? It was followed by *I'm sorry. I don't*
know what came over me. Don't tell anyone, please.

Sweating, I got in my car with my dog, put my
hands on the wheel and closed my eyes for a second,
and when I opened them I was surprised to
see that all the words had disappeared.

I took a deep breath, turned the ignition, and started home.

Landlady #1

It's a particular shade of pink
carbon dated with years
of stale coffee and cigarette smoke.
It's a pink that invites shuffling,
television in the background
and old ledgers on the plastic-covered
kitchen table.

Somewhere in the blue sequins
of the flickering across her eyes
she hates her reduction to light bulbs
and plungers, and "you're two
days late, when am I going
to get my check?" It sounds
like the old days.

It sounds like women she hears
on the bus, and she was one
of them once. Christ,
three kids and a cell phone
but no money for milk.
The butcher saves bones
for her watery soup. How does
a life become so small?

23 one-bedrooms stacked
like empty blocks and hers,
number 24, vacant
as a ghost ship in moonlight.
Nothing but the crossword
and furled calendar
to keep her counsel, her hands
dusted with time and words.

Landlady #8

She looks like a thrift shop
in a town of old women.
She has cats. More than three.

She sets her table for breakfast
every day, as if for unseen boarders,
never drinks from the carton,
wears ballet slippers always,
even to sleep.

She has dolls in original boxes,
hasn't had a date in 22 years,
owns not a single garment
of anything silk, her Jockeys
for Women white with blue
jonquils that only she sees.
She thinks "dress up" is something
you do for the doctor.

Matching her eye shadow to her sweater
you'd swear she's what happens
to small town cheerleaders when
life gluts them with regret, the way
her parents treated her and she's
used to it, the impudence of
not-cold-enough tap water,
flowers that fade in a day.

It's a sour and sad building
for lost souls and sheared-off
dreams. She navigates
between litter box and laundry,
checks the days off until Sunday,
prays for the villain on Telemundo
to come knocking, to beg for
sweet skin and hot tea

but she will not find him
in the market, her cart holds
not one luxury, nor condiment,
nor berries ripe with sun
to tempt him. She believes
he sends kisses but they are lost.
She unpacks her groceries,
changes the channel.

A Lesbian Named Virginia Stole My Chair

She said she's not a regular here
but she slid right into my chair as
if she were born there.

Jack and Coke in one hand,
a fingerful of frosting on her
other index finger,

she sipped and fed the frosting
to Tammi while listening to
a bad Blues singer wail about

right and wrong. Wrong was
her ass in my chair. But there never
was a sweeter kiss than

that frosting kiss, and when they left,
I felt as shriveled as the dried-up roses
forgotten on their table, waiting by the window.

Concerning the Concert

It was not the Debussy.

It was hearing the Debussy through your black hair, through that ear carved like a Hawthorne gable, through your eyes shaded like a bank teller frozen on the bill, through your mouth perched between smile and frown and the sigh you always bore at intermission.

When we listened on Thursday.

It was not her touch too heavy on the gliding key.

It was seeing her touch too staccato the keys and feeling your back slowly straighten and hearing the low grunt I only could hear and seeing your foot in the scratched black loafers glide closer to the torn seat in front of us and back, sudden back, in the same slow irritation.

When we sat still in the box on Thursday.

It was not the applause when she bowed in the blue strapless and gazed, quick gazed, at us.

It was seeing your streaked hands clap more slowly than the woman in the K-mart perfume who clapped it up in front of us and auditing the cramped, deliberate gesture as your one palm slowly glazed the other and seeing your legs cross, snap, as you glanced at your chipped Swiss watch.

The Thursday night we fought over the rent before the Debussy. And still. As we drank his *étude no. 4* in the box. And still, and still.

Large Poem Writ Small or Vice Versa

I

(what an obsessive pronoun that "I")

think about writing a P*O*E*M
writ large
with the Great Old Concepts
Beauty-Truth-Art
but this is the age of Sponge Bob Squarepants
Hannah Montana
zombies
and financial hysteria

the words are puny concepts
that worm across the PC screen
glowing
orange
now and then
but signifying nothing
but arbitrary ingenuity

and I talk too logically
that is subject-verb-object
to be postmodern
or post-language
where words spin out of control
like Darth Vader's little plane
at the end of Star wars Episode IV
which was really episode I

poetry
this poem at least
is a trivial pursuit
no beauty
even in a 1948 bathing suit
Atlantic City
Bess Myerson
gams that a gentle razor coveted

this poem is more like lust
than love

no discrimination in its sensibilities
and too abstract
like a commentary
for anyone hot and bothered and "cool"

this poem is so self-conscious
of its quasi-art
the plunking of words on a screen

not even paper now
not a notebook
no
the poet remotely types from a keyboard
no ink meshes into paper
no real experience gets into the words
just a lot of negation
running on at the mouth
happy to drool all over itself

is the poet or the poem
self-indulgent?
a rhetorical question
but this is too much like prose
too transparent
no strategy of camouflage
adjectives pecking and nicking at each other
like caged birds

I feed the words my ego
the language loves to eat me up
spit me out
refuse
for a poem
that sits in the alley
the can's lid not tightly on
a little to the side
the poet squinched up
in his own image
but not like a religious sacrifice
but like a bad loan

can't help making references
to the times
and the problems that point

their pea shooters at you
right in the eye
your net worth sinks
like the value of a post-modern poem
without Truth-Beauty-Art

it is just
truth
in blue jeans
holes at the knees

beauty
all covered
head to toe
with tapioca pudding
and some mafioso licking
illegal areas

art
dumped
a pile of dirt in a museum
and the landscape man
the guy who cuts the grass
is an artist
especially in protest
dumping clumps of dirt

what are we protesting?
God?
the Pope?
Nazi brutality?
Truth-Beauty-Art?
our own small concepts?
Pretentiousness?
Our own protests?

this is a post-modern poem
that
in the vernacular
sucks

if we were only babies. . . .

Underground Tubers

sometimes when I'm madly masturbating
I think about what it would be like
to be a man, to have a cock, this thick
hard piece of throbbing rubbery meat
swinging to and fro, bumping into things
insinuating itself into everything from love to lunch
my crazy imaginary penis has this need to
be pushed into things, pulled out of things
unclogging drains and investigating cisterns
waving traffic through intersections and
rescuing crying kittens treed in trees
and sometimes when I'm madly masturbating
I imagine the ecstasy of shoving that hard cock
into something alive, not just funnel cakes filled with fresh cream
not just flannel hats or leather shoes or scotch tape rolls
but something twitchy, and warm, and wet
what it would be like to ram and thrust
instead of always being the catcher

Something I Would Have Remembered Saying

I did not say to him, "I love you."
I may have mentioned how nicely
His suit matched his tie,

Or how brushing against his tight pecs
Submerged my senses. But, "I love you?"
That I would have remembered

Like the soldier who first made me surrender,
An olive-skinned, dark-maned lover
Whose solid hands turned my bed into a bema.

Perhaps I have been want for intimacy,
Something soft and whispery
Capable of consuming blue flames.

But I no longer attend those quick-fuck carnivals
Whose all-hard, all-the-time, lotharios
Require no ticket, no green, for admittance.

They say, "I love you" while opening a can of beer.
And happily do so again following a zephyr,
Something I could create by opening a window.

By metaphor did I say what he heard?
A touch to his shoulder? A sigh too strong?
Roiled with emotion I could have uttered a confession.

But not that. I lie with the sun in my eyes.
Into the penumbra a gray circling hawk laughs.
How I would have remembered telling him, "I love you."

Inner Works

We peddle our lives.
Like a hawker we shout out the benefits—
the emollients in the soap to soften
the razor-sharp blade that slices a tomato
paper-thin.

We peddle our wares without telling how
quickly the soap dissolves or how fast the
knife edge dulls. Instead we speak of fragrances
or catch a ray of light to reflect on the blade.
And although they fear the razor-edge,
they are captivated. They crave the fragrance
and the feel of pain.

To Ida

(pronounced Ee-dah) , 47 million year old fossil

Bless all star voyagers from the Messel Pit:
The small Creodont, early Pangolin,
Marsupials, lemur like prosimians,
Elegant early hedgehogs, jewel beetles,
The Messel bird, enigmatic combo of owl and hawk!
The Massillaropter, tiny hoopoes, hopping horses. . . .

Bless these fossils, but bless especially
Ee-dah- Darwinius Masillae, my Ida!
Who stood at a fork in the road pointing HUMAN!
Bless Ee-dah who for 47 million years
Until pulled from the quarry on a shale slab,
Slept dreaming—bless all travellers! I dream

Of a blue city in the distance—my home—
Purposeful, realized, I can see it
Far way in blue haze, Oz-like from this rest stop
On the thruway in the mountains—I can't get there!
No access to on ramp—stuck in the parking lot. . . .
Like Ida on her bier, resin around me like amber.

O strange sad condition—endless travel, suddenly stopping,
Never getting anywhere! Ee-dah were you heading
Towards the apes—humans or the lemurs?
O Ida, Ee-dah where are we going? in what direction?
The asphalt of parking lots a calm, dark blue,
The blue city on the plains mirage blue.

Theory of Travel I

What you want is childhood—
not childhood but its sensations

everything new and unfamiliar.
For this you'd travel far:

stairs stacked like precarious
piles of books, strings of vines

rappelling down sheer cuts,
terror of the tidal pull of crowds.

You are not the informed traveler,
armed with names and dates

and some useful phrases,
for whom destination is validation.

You like to travel unprejudiced
by expectation, in spite of the risk

or because of the risk: will
the world catch you when you fall?

You peel off your identities,
leave your bags in the stuffy hotel

room with the crippled ceiling fan,
and stride onto the playground

of the senses, eager to be whirled
in the mad dance of competing cries,

the jangle of bells and gold bangles,
screeching, long-tailed birds on sticks.

You wade into a profusion of
flowers: what's that yellow one,

that red spiky one, the one
with petals like goldfish fins?

Everything stripped to primer simplicity:

flower, yellow, red, fish.

Nameless, nameless—everything
without a history of experience,

your once-reliable senses
unmoored by caterpillars

that look like flowers, shells
like teeth, moss like sandpaper.

Suddenly the street becomes
a blurred wash of colors;

you hear a cloud of music
with a heavy clash of odors. . . .

A woman is propping you up
saying something insistently,

holding a cup to your lips.
Without hesitation, you drink.

Imagining Eternity

You were asking me about eternity,
which always calls up images of immense
space suffused with a golden glow
and a sense of unreality.

I was looking out the window absently
into the dusk, wondering how
to answer and tired of imponderables.

Far across the valley
a dog barked
and filled the evening
with loneliness,
and I ached for this world.

How I loved it:
the wrinkled green skirts of the mountains
enfolding the nestlings and the secret prowlers,

the pastel houses and plain gray ones
all huddled together for companionship,
the trees spreading umbrella-like over them.
And beyond, the Pacific stained orange
with the juice of the sun it eats entire
every evening, and the opaque waters' vastness
as much as I can imagine of eternity.

Bedroom

Bed-room, with or without a hyphen or spelt backwards,
is a sketch from a ten year old with curtains drawn. Outside,

a primrose sun casts rays over a stiff chimney pot. Mother
and Father are matchstick people with arms outstretched. Fingers

separate widely to show the blue of continuous sky. A door can
be barricaded. A hiding place under the bed rates

among the most cobwebbed spots in the world. Forget
the onus on us to *rise and shine*—a bed-room is a place

of white, netted curtains hanging on a drooping wire. A trailer
of turf blocks the view and white netting becomes a wedding veil tied

in a knot at the nape of a neck. A *Sacred Heart* light with a bulb fused
is the only audience. Imagine the stillness of a bedspread mummifying

a body. The height of the ceiling gags a mouth. The Top 20 crackles
from a fallen radio. Abba's *Dancing Queen* skirts a thousand issues.

An ear pressed against a mattress feels the weightlessness of goose-
        down.
Spittle escaping from the side of a mouth, if left long enough, can drown

a fly. In a bedroom, tears can well up and cover the story
of *Noah's Ark* where everything has a match. Moving in twos

or the arithmetic of two never completely unhinges light-footed
ghosts that ceaselessly self-reflect in bedroom door handles.

The People One Meets While Wearing a Hat

Graham and my husband met while my husband was wearing
a red-star, Vietnamese, canvas hat. My husband was between two
pier walls, fishing, and sheltering from the wind that had lifted
the plastic chair from underneath the old lady who had bent
forward to shake sand from her shoe. I met Graham while wearing
a woolly hat and looking for light under a street lamp. Graham

had every gadget one could imagine—hook sharpeners, braces

for waders and a life jacket that came to midriff. Graham was staying
with his ex-wife who attempted suicide on both Christmas Eve
and New Year's Eve. Graham fished as if his life depended on it.
He spoke about a type of fish that had teeth in its fins; once he stood
talking to his ex-wife with fingers bleeding while holding the fish

the wrong way round. Octopuses changed colours in his fridge,
on the grass verge and on the back seat of his car. Graham confessed
he once had a girlfriend who was a nymphomaniac. He searched
in his breast pocket for a photo of a female employee who was beautiful,
worked hard but rolled joints at 8 am. Graham always bought warm
bread in the mornings. I saw him buy warm bread on the morning

that Saddam Hussein's execution photo appeared in the newspaper.
Graham said he would drink anything, even methylated spirits but
instead he drank a bottle of red wine and a bottle of white wine and left
our house with a bucket of stale bread at 4 am. Graham did not outstay
his welcome, nor did he ever wear a hat, not in all the time we knew
him.

Homecoming Tallahassee

We passed into the city
like sterile vessels
aching under the 3 o'clock hour.
Our eyes staggered through
the epileptic cop car lights,
picking still freeze scenes
from the festival blur.
Loud rice cake voices, singing blandly,
motored by, while bass-lines
bucked the soft, dark fat
of the night's underbelly.
The town was an echo
of beastly thundering.
Alley cat eyes prowled
in aimless acquisition.
Traffic jammed,
bumper-bumper rut
thumped on the gas.
Booming happy swarms
bounced off our headlights.
Gaping past the cranking cars,
I saw the quiet moon shudder in the sky.

Café Luna

You pool in excess,
liquid as the light
puddled on the fading
velvet of the chair.
Like a nervous
squirrel pawing
a nut,
you touch your queen,
and the room corners me
until I feel like a funny
puzzle in which the pieces
have been forced together.
My eyes,

dim, milkless
saucers,
counter yours.
Around us, voices
dribble and caffeine
lips are glued to
rattling coffee mugs,
but I hear only your fingers crawling.
A sudden arm
tips the table and
a black knight becomes
a casualty.

Blowtorch

The older kids at camp show us how.

I can't always hear
what it is they're saying,

only the grave, conspiratorial tone
in which they say it.

But when the spray from the can
hits the flame of the Bic lighter,

Hiroshima!

I look around—mountains, a river,
the suggestion of a sun.

And so many things to burn.

The Morning After

I know the sound of a fist striking flesh
In the night, through a bedroom door shut tight.
And her quiet, tearful pleading—no, no,
No. No bruises, just internal bleeding.

Eating a breakfast of anguish at a
Round, faux-wood Formica table. Cupboards
Stocked with terror. I kept my heart in an
Avocado green refrigerator.

Safe from the simmering pot on the stove,
To soon boil over, even unprovoked.
I'd quietly rinse my cereal bowl,
Take my game-face from the closet, and go.

Mornings—she swept spent ashes of rage. Steeped
Guilt in a tea cup, and sipped it away.

two holy men

the two holy men
come into the library every day
when i'm working the ref desk
and answering the same questions
i always have to answer
or biding my time before
i have to toss our regular drunk
off of his computer
for swearing at old muhammad ali
boxing matches again
and taking hits off a pint of smirnoff.
but the two holy men
they have this routine
where they pick through all of
the free pencils until they've found
the sharpest ones
then they take piles of scrap paper
and sit right next to each other
where they spend the next two hours
drawing pictures of the bible and chalices
with the crucifix illuminated above the golden cup.
the two holy men are meticulous in this
they draw the same things over and over again
and the drawings are almost exact each time
with small variations that maybe you'd
be able to see if you had a trained eye.
it is insanity and genius incarnate.
and the only problem i ever have with them
is that one of the holy men thinks it's a good idea
to hang his drawings up all over the library
and if i'm not paying attention
they'll be drawings of chalices and bibles
all over the children's department and bathroom
sketches shoved in with paperbacks
and self-help books
and the two holy men will be out the door
off to who knows where
to converse again with god
and i'll have to get up and go around the library
throwing away all of the drawings

of bibles and chalices
with crucifixes illuminated above the golden cup
as if it were my divine and designated right to do so.

Shattered Fetlock

My uncle tells me not to
touch the tiny blue eggs
nested in the oleander bush

outside his front door.
His doorbell sounds
like a fading ice-cream

truck. Robins congregate
on his lawn, singing a Beatle's
album in reverse. On the front

steps I wear heavy gloves
meant for a much larger
man, but everything is breaking,
opening its yellow eyes.

This Road Goes South

Construction in the woods
again keeps me up all night.

Someone has left a baby there,
and men are trying to find it;

pitchforks, shovels, specially
trained terriers with squeals

that sound like angels crying.
The lights themselves have

a noise, a rough engine hum.
Remember when I fell into the well

when I was four? I still have the scar
on my forehead. I think of that opening

dark every time your tail lights dim,
further and further into the trees.

At 101

all that could be done
has been done already

what had to be done
she did

years ago

past becomes future
in her ears

say: *I'm going to see
Loretta in Atlanta*

get: *I bet she was
surprised to see you*

in return

nothing to look forward to
but the past

those gone over
to the other side

returned
to take her

home.

Eugene Bullard, Descending

Piloting captains of the airwaves,
you rise 70, 80, 100 floors
but go no higher, get nowhere
every day, day after day, over
and over, week in, year out.
As if you never were a Columbus
fleeing Georgia, zig zagging across
Europe, once Le Grand Duc du Jazz,
master of the square ring, or the

Black Swallow of Death in the skies
over France. Beneath the well-pressed
uniform, no one sees your medalled heart
still burning like the star-filled night,
the sharp eye sill capable of keeping secrets
beneath the tip of a polished cap.

Your flame still burns in Paris, free.
America had a left hook you didn't
see coming to set you back into
what it called your place—
just another black man in a box
going down.

> *Awarded the Croix de Guerre for his bravery at the Battle of
> Verdun, Eugene Bullard (1895–1961) was the first black com-
> bat aviator, flying twenty missions for the French Air Corps and
> downing at least one German plane. In the late 1930s Bullard
> joined a French government counterintelligence network spy-
> ing on Germans in Paris. When the Nazis conquered France in
> 1940, Bullard escaped to New York City with his family, where
> he worked in a variety of occupations, including his final job as
> an elevator operator at the RCA Building in Rockefeller Center.*

The Music of Scott Joplin From Original Piano Rolls

> *These entertainments are not art. They excite like machines, animals,
> landscapes, danger.*
> *– Jean Cocteau*

Finally, you get to show them what you mean:
*Do not play this fast. It is never right to play
Ragtime fast.* If anything, the machine with its
clicking pens and electrical connections slows you
down even further, forces more precision, reveals
more from the jagged rhythms than most would catch
at normal speeds. More than most want to hear.

The engineer leans in to notate the dynamics of
your variations. the weight of your dark body
too heavy for America's formal chairs. Instead

they will create a ghostly presence in their parlor
from an absence—rectangular holes cut into a long
white roll. Remain invisible and you are a welcome
light touch emanating from the corner.

No matter. Press down on the keys, create the black
marks later to be struck through the thick paper
to make sound. you are playing to some other place,
some different time, where you are more than just
the King of Ragged Time, but known for weaving
complex dreams and heartache into song, for the strange
turns in the tertiary melody: melancholy, intelligent,
introspective, as if someone caught a sudden glimpse of

a lone wall flower at the summer dance, waiting alone but proud,
knowing her turn will come, not yet, not now, but soon.

Out of Town

(for *Christopher Stackhouse*)

Everyone there reminds you of someone else—
that woman in the hotel bar's the girl
you sat next to in kindergarten, those people

across the street look like the couple with four
bikes you helped outside Wal-Mart last Christmas.
The guy at the gas station always begging change

is here transformed into a banker, the bus driver
your first disastrous blind date in school. Names
gather at the tip of the tongue, refusing to go further.
Even you,

you no longer look like yourself here,
but that other guy, that actor, singer, football player,
the priest who married your friend's sister. The hoodlum
everyone mistakes you for.

Walking dusk's quiet, rolled up streets,
you peer into glowing houses at set-for-dinner tables,
the backs of empty chairs, a flickering TV set

at the end of a long hall illuminated by long-held and–lost desires,
stare through the mirrored glass, searching for
the life you could have lead.

"Self"

for Douglas Kearney

A black man's got to have a private world.
    "The Black and White Galaxie" – Afaa Michael Weaver

Dark mirror

smooth
empty template

without center
eternal foil

continuous
contingent masquerade

rising
being born—

or is it
iceberg

true mass
below the surface

under view
beyond review

every
thing

everyone wants
to see

staring from
pitch black

sanded

surface:

A mirrored dark

> *Martin Puryear: Self, 1978, stained and painted red cedar and mahogany, National Gallery of Art, Washington DC*

Encumbrances Of Angels

With all eternity to ponder
the nature and cost of freedom,
even an angel might prefer
the rasp of sand between the toes
to the ethereal tug of cosmic tides,
choose the angularity of starfish
over the symmetry of stars,
desire—whatever the penalty—
the lash of wind-driven rain
on a back unburdened of wings.

To The Heart In Its Dark Cavern

> *Take down the dulcimer.*
> *Let the beauty we love be what we do.*
>   *–Rumi*

A time comes in any mourning to strip away
the black and throw open the windows.
Remembrance lingers, a scent like lilacs,
a delicate cameo on a dark velvet ribbon.

But stubborn, so stubborn, the heart protests:
it has been embalmed with the beloved dead.
Timid, swathed in layered black crepe,
what else is it to think? Love might persist
like water, but cleansing takes time.

Gradual changes: carry the morning cup
of tea into the garden, pick three wildflowers.
Observe the subtle truths of trees
and the evocative quiet of stones.
For now, song contentedly reposes
in an unopened drawer with the good silver.

Later, take down the dulcimer, blow off the dust.
Go slowly. Know the malarial, wrenching fevers
will recur. Polish the instrument, replace strings,
tune. Be patient, and more than patient,

until that day when silence begs for music
and the fingers ache to pluck the strings.

Grandfather's Clock

I wonder how many little girls
spent cozy evenings
with their daddies,
counting,
binding
the thick, ecru coupons
that came in packs of Raleighs;
looking through the catalogues,
circling all the things that
they dreamed about buying,
and maybe were proud
when the grandfather's clock
bought from a million or so packs
arrived on the doorstep.
I wonder how many teens
on the edge of womanhood
rushed home to beat the chiming clock
when curfew came too soon,
and instead of going inside
would sit with Dad on the front stoop,
watching
the red tip flash
as he inhaled deeply,
then blew smoke into the air.
And they'd talk,
about everything,
nothing,
watching fireflies in the loblolly pines.
I wonder how many women,
maybe some with kids of her own,
stopped winding the clock
when there wasn't enough time,
with, you know,
radiation
and trying to wipe his hair
out of the tub
before he showered again.
How many women
stopped dusting it—
Even though it needed dusting,

Even though it sat at the head of his
hospital bed
in the living room—
knowing exactly what *you can get*
from smoking Raleighs.

A Traveler Taken Into the Hands of the Moon

A Greyhound traveler on a winter
night fallen dirty drunk
onto a conch shell seat.

The bus cautious, silent
like a Huron bride raiding party.

Cities black as London in the blitz.
Early snow, the road not yet closed,
snowplows hunched like crows on a wire.

My home town passes outside
the black sea of the window.

High school
and all my unlearned French.
The marriage, marine service
and coming home
young.

Divorce
discussed like ordering a meal.
Property divided
on the back of a napkin.

Days slip their leash.
Birds change tint,
lift off for southern states.

I drift, idle, a man without
work. Life pissed into a

corner; under a cerulean sky
the moon sags into the rose glove
of the earth's quarter dark.

The Handsomest Man in Cuba

I talk to you like a small town editor pounding his typewriter late at night, or the handsomest man in Cuba singing at the Hotel Nacional in a white dinner jacket and bow tie, or an architecture student lazing at the Malecon seawall, smoke drifts to Havana, the heat and boredom so heavy and this blackness from the window, my yellow Desoto rests faithfully below and a passing train far off whistles with ripe bananas and tins of condensed milk, I cannot think straight...

The office empty, the broiling sky scooped into rainless clouds between the farms, the green tractor in the stubble field where you read my letter,

the scalding, truck-watered streets where you thumb my epistle by the one street light, a room where you dance

with a heavy woman whose name I do not know, your barracks, your bus,
your shaking boat headed to Florida,

I'm speaking to you, the resolutions, the relentless exhortations on our black and white TV. Excuse my desolation, my unkempt apperance.

Trips to harvest the cane by students, the stumbling, rusted taxis, the eternal sacrifice and doing without, the lying to ourselves

about our importance, the medical school and broken x-ray machine, broken sides of every building, broken sidewalks on broken streets.

Wind on the corrugated roofs of the one room farmhouses, my words in the dripping tomatoes, the hand painted rocking chairs and garden poinsettias.

You veteranos in the colonial square over dominoes, shirts dry in the limp air above your white hair—your carbine still oiled from the Sierra Maestra.

How often I stumble no longer believing in the collective, but the commonweal shimmers, a friend holding the hand of a friend.

The entire generation sacrificed and set aside as a newspaper truck returns with unsold copies.

I cannot think straight, sick with the disease of having nothing, the power poles without power, laws made in secret, my oration for the fallen dead,

false reports of spies listening at soccer fields, whispers and the snoozing grumble of half-fed

boys, yes I see you thinking of a crime, demanding a voice from the patched telephone, clutching your spare white undershirt.

The haze of cooking oil, the *vereda tropical* of food smells—our path of cooking beans and scented rice—-fraternal order of cooking pans.

The reader by a low watt bulb, light crust of mildew in the old walls and hallways, the stiffening limb of a flower in a window pot.

The flight into reverie and remembrance, looking homeward where home no longer exists.

The aloneness to which the aging embargo condemns my island, whiskered young men sit dumbfounded, silently weeping

into the green Caribbean breakers, women of plumbed sepia open their arms humming.

Rune

I want the nineteenth century today—
to whirl the globe of time back, say,
one-hundred-thirty years—1879's soft,
careful and precise locutions—a fantasy
and sway to which my mind gives play
when winter light is like it is right now: before
it makes another shy diffusely glowing bow

into the evening—Emily Dickinson, 48,
and Henry James at 35, arrive—appositely
at my desk for ghostly tea, but each quite
quickly takes an interest in the other—not
in me: Henry's gray and Emily's dark sherry
eyes inspect their captive prey and prize—
dispassionate, direct—as if they each

were insect specimens; I want to waft
my deftest sweetest clauses for them
into meaning—elegant and filigreed,
but simple as the simplest human breath—
I want the bliss of thinking I might get their
blessing—but they're too bewildered by
each other to address another being—dusk

slowly swallows both—and I'm back here
one-hundred-thirty years beyond the hush
of their improbable encounter and existence.
Cell phone shocks the air: a friend calls:
have to meet him soon. I trudge into the cold
Manhattan evening: half-moon—whispered
utterance—etched, peculiar as a rune.

The Weight of One Small Death

When I lifted the dead sparrow
from the lawn, it was light,
incredibly light: lighter
than a sheet of paper; lighter
than the bird alive; nearly lighter
than the weight in hand,
which was light—light
as the thought of a bird.

United States Soldiers in Italy—End of World War II

It was paradox even to those who did know the word.
Stretched out, the Tuscan hills—the fields of wheat
and lavender, vines that took root
before the Romans came, when the Etruscans
lived and farmed beneath this sun;
buildings ancient when American was formed;
clustered towns where the horde of years
gave dignity to roofs and privy stalls—
yet here rivers of blood had flowed
and countless battles raged.
Even after the Italians surrendered the Germans fought on:
Anzio, Monte Cassino, the massacre at Saint Anna de Stazzena;
and Mussolini and his woman hung up by their feet and shot;
the Jews captured, detained, then herded off to Auschwitz.
Here in the land of food, of beauty, art, and hospitality,
levies broke and death spilled out in flood.

Some knew, of course, this was the root of Rome:
forge of short-swords, dye-vat of red capes
that signified violence and tyranny
around the sea they called "our sea" and north
to Gaul and Britain, east to the Euphrates.
A few miles from where they were garrisoned,
the Florentines betrayed, murdered and fought.
Dante's bitter exile came from here;
the mercenary Englishman Hawkwood
(the Italians called him the devil incarnate)
rode down these roads. All raised their swords.
But roses climb the rough-hewn walls
one time besieged, and poppies blossom in the battlefields.
It seems remote, history a made-up tale.

The guns are quiet. The stunned silence
of what has been
falls down like dust and makes rejoicing sad.
Ecstatic celebration quickly fades
when legions of the dead march back
into their memories: those whom they knew
and slept beside, ate with, sweated beside

in battle; or the ones they never knew—real ghosts
whose deaths dotted the hills of Italy
just as flowers dotted hills, lined paths.

They will exchange the sleepy Tuscan fields
for Indiana, Michigan, New York.
Yet Italy will lodge in their remembrance.
Here they learned beauty and death entwine—
the poisoned plant lodged in the lily path,
the serpent coiled at the lovely maiden's feet,
the unseen plague riding the fragrant wind.

Reflections on My Son's Twenty-Fifth Birthday

June 3, 2009

There is a wound that every man must heal,
inflicted by his father. It may come
from anger or ambition or the zeal
to see his longings realized in his son;
it may arise from dreams he had to leave
behind but thinks his boy can salvage them,
show up at the last hour to reprieve
his failure, the goals that eluded him;
it may be drunkenness or bullying,
withdrawal or bitterness—a myriad
of subtle injuries fathers can bring
to make their sons bitter, angry, or sad.

I only hope the years, in passing, see
healing of hurts, wholeness of memory.

Grieving

I seem to be grieving
        For my mother, my father, my son,
        For my brothers and others,
        For myself prematurely,
        For the life I might have led—

Such futility! Not that we do not
        Deserve to be remembered,
        Mourned,

But the last is certainly not finished,
        And who knows
        The mistakes yet to be made.

Body Talk

The witch taps head and chest
with long fingers and mutters *thyroid, thymus,*
presses down the resisting arm.

10AM or 4PM which does your body want,
I'm better at 4 she says but the group
from Cincinnati wants a demo in the morning.

Bony face, big nose, black eyes:
taps like a hungry chicken, mutters
grief, grief, and I know I'm in the right place—

This witch has got something for me.

Asclepias

Milkweed butts up against the power
substation's concrete vehicle barrier,
added after 9/11 to supplement
the hurricane fence capped with razor wire.
The gangly plant reaches above the wall,
trying to get its share of
the dawn sun. Under its leaves,
hoping a maintenance man doesn't
get ideas of RoundUp, lie eggs. They wait
for their own Kafka experience of
eventual monarchhood. Their births'
main ambition... a flight to Mexico.
A fluttering black and orange
prayer to the ephemeral.

Hara-kiri

> *How sad, to think that even fire*
> *ends in aimless smoke—- "Shunzei's Daughter"*

In a garden filled with plum trees,
lemon and chrysanthemum,
Nagata kneels, adjusting his kimono.

The folds of white and yellow silk
are perfectly arranged to complement
the budding colors of the evening clouds.

He contemplates the blade before him
gathering the waning sunlight,
the ivory handle, carved by Hanshumori,

worth a thousand fortunes—
so delicate!—displayed upon
a crimson pillow at his knees.

All the victories and glory
he delivered to his lord, Yamura,
have brought him to these rites.

It is the peasants that he blames—
as they are blamed for everything—
they cheered him louder than his lord.

"Your *seppuku* shall be your reward,"
so said old Yamura, presenting him
this dagger he will own an afternoon.

The bright blade's touch against his thumb
brings ruby droplets gently to the silk.
He turns to his retainer, poised behind,

two hundred year old sword in hand,
and tells him, "Not too quickly;
do not strike until the third incision."

Two men alone within a garden,
crowded with a thousand year's tradition.
He stares into the blossoms, seeking clarity,

awaiting inspiration for his death-haiku.
Nagata notes a slight disturbance in a plum tree—
a sparrow, laboring to build its nest...

"Industrious sparrow,
build fast your empire of twigs...
leaves falling"....

His attendant nods in admiration.
The words will be remembered.
And now the clouds are hyacinth and jade,

rose-pink and vermilion. He grasps
the ivory handle, opens his kimono
and thrusts. The unexpected pain

sears him like a firestorm. He pulls
the blade across—the second movement—
realizing that the shock

has robbed him of his strength.
He cannot slant the blade up to his ribs.
A shout, a scream, conceived within his lungs

is crawling up his chest, now running
for his throat—a rush of air behind—
then all is black, the garden gone,

his stillborn scream a murmured breeze,
a slight disturbance of the leaves
of a plum tree, where a sparrow builds its nest.

Somewhere Between

> *I've seen...attack-ships on fire, off the shoulder of Orion.*
> *I've watched C-beams glitter in the dark near the Tannhauser Gate.*
> *All those moments will be lost in time, like tears in rain.*
> *– from the film Blade Runner*

Somewhere
between the whisky and the prayers
there comes a time...

although for earnest seasons
you've changed your coat, your colors;
summer sable, winter white...

a time—in spite of all your tyings, your un-tyings—
will come with sword in hand like Alexander,
cut the knots, take your careful fingers with them.

There comes a time you know
grace has leaked out of the reliquary.
Open it and see the spider—dead black button,

once leafy legs now folded up, a dried umbrella,
no longer threatening; no longer real.
It may take a while, may wear a low velocity,

like some green disease boring to the center of the earth;
but, eventually, the cat does *not* come back.
Eventually even Odysseus knows it's time to go home...

and there you are, standing in the mall,
staring at the young girls in their tight jeans walking by,
like starships bursting into flame off the shoulder of Orion.

There you are, reduced, judged in two dimensions, some
jackal-headed Romeo on a ruined temple wall, the weight
of your soul somewhere between a feather and the world.

The Great Blue Heron

I stand at the window, a shadow,
as the heron soars down from daylight
and lands in the lake, a statue.
Perfectly still with grey-blue feathers,
his stilts leave no ripples in the water;
the world remains undisturbed.
He stands ready with stoic patience,
waiting for movement in the shallows,
striding with careful placement
until his long, graceful neck darts down
and his chopstick beak captures a fish.
He soars off, a reflection,
only the fish and me
ever knowing of his existence
as he floats effortlessly on air
towards the shore.

Praying Mantis

for Dottie May

I should have known
when the magnolias died in frost
that it would be her last spring—
the way the blossoms hung on for weeks,
brown and wilted, shrouding the house
with their flitting petal shadows.

She had taken to wandering the yard
as if surveying the inches of grass
and patches of garden, each flowering plant
she had tended these fifty years. She no longer
called to me across the fence
to show me something of beauty—
a budding hydrangea, a ripening fig

or a praying mantis
crouched among daffodils,
perched on its forelegs
in a position of total alertness,
total tranquility.

Cicadas

From under the earth, like lava, like oil,
like boiling water through a geyser,
they emerge

From seventeen years of darkness
beneath our feet, from that humming
from feeding on roots

they push through the surface
to sunlight, tree trunks,
telephone poles, flower stems

where they cling and wait,
sing and wait.

Rapture

Applaud the lovers,
who have no worldly riches to bestow,
who climb the attic stairs
with only their bodies to give,
where the bed,
a soiled mattress on the floor awaits them—
their torsos bathed in moonlight,
the night air at their backs.

Their time under the stars
reason enough to fall
headlong into each other's desires—
not for them the sweet talk of posterity,
nor the bitter talk of betrayal.
Applaud the lovers, dumb before God
and holy man,
with only their youth to live for.

Washed Up

Though it was only one myth of the birth of Venus that said She was
    born conceived not out of love but springing full-grown from the
    sea,
I combed the strand to try to find what aspect of salt water the myth-
    maker must have had in mind that it should bear Love, or Beauty,

collecting Ocean's detritus: jellies' stingers, anemones, chipped shells, a
    smashed-in nautilus, the filmy foam like ambergris.
The waves beat like a metronome on Largo, rushing, reversing, rewash-
    ing with a polychrome the stones and sands. And everything

destroyed or dying in the sands looked beautiful. As suddenly it washed
    away. I washed my hands, my legs, my head, then all of me—
that She might reach my soul, my heart—by leaping in a swelling roar.
    Instead She tore me half apart washing twisted limbs ashore.

But in the breaker I recall the violent rinsing off of half a sorry life,
    egesting all my past in one great gurgling laugh.
When stragglers, who are out to comb the beach as I have been, find me
    they'll say my body, swaddled in foam, glistens, almost beautifully.

Miss Lee

   Peggy Lee, 1920 – 2002

She had the cognac voice, the brandy breast,
the corrugated heart, as iron as
the mullion giving panes the strength to hold.
A bout of Fever gave her discernible flaws,
a nick in the ribbing, a bubble in the glass.

But how she fought. How many comebacks can
you count to? The one Goodman in her life
died young, but she sang on, ran off, sang on,
and disappeared, then crooned and wrote again.
Now the iron, the glass, the ribs, the bubbles, are gone.

I have but one of her, in vinyl, scratched,
and set it spinning on the turntable,

sitting by my window with a shot
of something, wondering Is that all there is?—
then pour another, wishing it were not.

The Hand of God

(after Rodin's The Hand of God)

Pools. Rocks. Chunks of time.
Switches on the trees and animals
walking around, stripped to their walking,
naked, shivering, lissome in their pelts.
They began as the apparition of a gesture,
a shrinking itself as wide as the void,
until I had made my whole self a hand
to apprehend my own loneliness
as easily as one picks up a stone
from an otherwise unpopulated shore
and carries it back, a portable barrenness.
And I began to love myself
until the clay pulsed
like a navel into which has burrowed
a small, lively insect.
Theirs was a crawling birth.
And when I saw them
I thought the world had flickered
and spun itself into their singular embrace.
And when I saw that their liberal forms
had grazed on the light,
I grew jealous and struck them,
and from under my palm
there moved a shadow—the first!—
I now call regret.

Housecleaning

There's two lives:
one you live through, one you don't.
As you frisk your clothes of lint,
scour pans of last night's grease,
dust the banisters with an oiled cloth,
vacuum crumbs from under the loveseat,
and beat the rugs till your arms ache
like a new mother's, you sense

you are putting things to right.
How will your life look without you in it?
Glimpse it: the clotted scum that rings the tub
is gone, the tiny, cauliflower impressions of lipstick
are wiped clean from the cups, and the dishes,
brightly rimmed, shine like new snow in the cabinet.
The house is innocent as a baby's skull,
and yet it is a brittle equilibrium.
You don't want to disturb it
with your body's tireless sheddings,
its particulate tattle-telling, its ways
of weaving its tarnishing signatures
through and on whatever you touch, hold, handle, use
or simply slump in or on. And you wonder
which life you have chastened
with your scrubbing, sweeping, and polishing,
which life you have ground down into a fine, blue essence
like the powder they use to make
stained glass windows.
You examine your hands
and see that the transference of grit and grime
is already framing you as the fraudulent
practitioner of the art of erasure.
You rest your fingertips on the white molding,
and a mark is made.
In the waning light it looks like the noseprint
of a small, stubborn ghost.
You decide to go on living.

librarian in chinatown

she's a librarian
but you hear bongos whenever she walks by
she wears those nylons, the ones with the seams
sweet jesus those seams
that lead you like a dog on a leash

i was looking for some mystery
i could feel sheila's marble grey eyes
staring into the back of my head
through the gap between gardner and hammett
she was always hanging around
in her white cashmere sweater and black rimmed glasses
suggesting some title, usually by mickey spillane

kiss me deadly?
have you ever read kiss me deadly?
no, i haven't but i'll get around to it
thanks sheila

nice kid but a little spooky
i was hearing those bongos again
this time with a hint of patchouli
the librarian was walking towards
the room where they keep the books
that don't cut it anymore
two chinese guys dressed in sharkskin suits
followed her into the withdrawal shelves
I heard footsteps from behind
as I took a dive into a dark deep pool...

sir, excuse me, sir
but the library closes in five minutes
must have dozed off
sweet jesus those seams...

June 16th 1984—Birthday

The same morning I discovered Plath
And Hughes wed on my birthday, my sister's
Too, I started reading Birthday Letters, trudged
In record snows with slight fever, missed the train, lost
You and wrote a poem beginning I am broken
Like glass bottles'—which talks of red eyes
Pointless ripostes, wrong turnings and black holes;
The, poker-hot, cinders of troubled minds.

On my 22nd I flew to Delhi, bussed it to Vashist
Chasing you that cut me loose, from where I hung
Content as plant in basket. It could have been
Jerusalem, Jaffna, Jupiter, I'd still have gone,
Still have packed my things inside the bag I borrowed
With adrenalins and stomach sirens blaring:
To red dust tika sunrise, through brimming bead market
Where henna printed hands contort for rupees
Amongst new shades of Himalayan
Light and dark.

Within 6 short months of this rescue mission
I'd coined a whole new fleet of commotions
And there, subverted, you found yourself
In the driver's seat, of a crashing plane
Or thrashing bull (*on a good day*).
No panic button, no safety harness
So I understand, the gone for good'
At Christmas, then once more the year following
When the torment came flooding back
Like the panic of blindness under water
Like the fear of drowning.

You were all directions, plugged
Into my live currents, panacea for poorest
Attributes. Perhaps that's not completely true
But it roughly fits and *I am* left curious,
Where should I varsity, now my poetry
Can't take your charity hand-in-hand?
Skip together, to where they're housed together
To where they bleed and cry, unjudged
Like things newborn, battling enormity

From their opposite corners.

I remember my 16th, unwrapping Ulysses
To discover Bloomsday too, on June 16th
Clapped eyes on a brochure boasting
Dublin's literary zenith': join penchants
Of language for Irish lore, dancing
Twirling jig, slip, single-treble-step
To a 6/8 metre, eat sausage pudding
Single-treble measure, roost
And read in races, voice blasting
Open-air, Celtic singsonging.

How I yearn to be clean, unharmed
Harmless; before the heart's chambers
Were loaded, dangerous like drunks with pistols.
Fully promise, I never knew what was coming
At 18, iron willed, I thought I had it made
This terse gospel and I had found a nest, above
The tower blocks and tombstones and dark trees
Bearing fruit. These chewable totems, fixed
All towns' broken yolks. And then, I saw it
Crow-black, gaping shadow...
.....In *my* sun.

After The Evening Lecture On Insight Meditation

I walked under a sky glowing indigo,
past pine trees giving off the last
of their warm scent.
I came home to my husband,
twirled in my long skirt
beside the still-cluttered kitchen sink
while in the living room our daughter
was up way beyond bedtime.
I had no urge to scold anyone.
She scurried to her piano,
I heard her hands
release the *Ode to Joy*.

A Poet in Winter

I'm still here,
hovering in a white
dominion—not that of Emily's
wardrobe—

but blank pages,
and windows encrusted
with a cold too hard
to scrape clear.

Even Keats needed a thrush or two
to get the blood of ink to flow,
even he wanted some rose-tinged field of autumn
to set him to enduring flame.

In Yaya's Den

In previous incarnations, it was
my mother's teenage bedroom,
my young aunt's refuge after divorce.
In my time, we gathered after supper for *Gunsmoke,*

I Love Lucy on the black and white console TV
that stood beside her ancient Singer
where my sister and I had carved
our names in the wood.

Id sit beside my grandmother, watching
her hands that refused to stay empty
since her 3-year-old son
died in that life before mine.
I took for granted her fingers' constant motion
of creation, the copper crochet hook dipping through
the yarn: another astonishing afghan born
on her blue knubby couch as she worked;
she sat at the end, leaning toward the strongest light.

Dry Spell Coming

Don't tell me the branches
have stopped announcing green—

that the spigot now drips
brown rust to the tile.

Don't tell me that lush moon
in my window has already
turned its face,

that what the guidebook said
about the home of the great dead
poet is true: even
the nightingales are gone—

don't tell me that.

Listening To A Recording Of Contemporary Poets
I Wonder

what Emily Dickinson would sound like—

a field mouse
murmuring behind a pantry wall,

or the skin of a cosmos seed
cracking open under soil?

Perhaps something more wintry—

crystals blooming on a pane, just as the moon
breaks through behind them,

as the dusty tail of a comet
melts into the indelible dark.

First Fall Semester

I bounded off the Badger Bus, grinning
at my best friend Cassie ready
to show me the way to the Bakers Rooms.
A line wound out the door; we didn't mind
waiting; classes would not start for a week.
We took a spiral staircase down
into the bowels of the vintage brick
building. Chandeliers hung low.
Vivialdi's strings filled the air,
and coffee smells like brown rich peat.
Linen flowed over small round tables
set with silver, crystal pots heaped
wth glistening jam we lathered over
our warm croissants. Even the steam
tasted of butter. And the jam, oh
the jam that crunched gently in our mouths
was studded with seeds like those
Persephone tasted after she left
her world, when she knew
she would never return home to stay.

Sun Lover

Face upturned, arms and legs
splayed out in tall grass,
I could be a plant taking light,
making it food,

warmth seeping through skin,
flesh on the verge
of some joyful, chemical
transformation.

I think of the faithful
who open their mouths for the wafer
dissolving, converting
to something like god in their bodies.

when asked to paint the world

when asked
to paint
the world

through the eyes
of
a terrorist

the painter
began

detailing
homes and
people

office buildings
and airplanes

school buildings and
churches

the vision was
almost finished

the way
she thought

it ought
to be

and when the last
stroke was done

she stepped
away

and lit
the canvas on fire.

Masque

To begin small: the vireo and his whisper song,
        courting from the sweetgum tree.
Not the loud proclamation proclaiming the self.
Not the blustery masque of shrill notes piercing
           the woods but:
leaning close and *nearly* speaking,
          as though words
are wild fruit that sag and sag but cannot bring
          themselves to fall.
To stand so near sometimes
it is a sky growing heavier and heavier
(wet air
        would drown you if it knew how).
The vireo calling into the woods like a single
leaf falling from the highest sweetgum limb.
        You look up and it is
drifting toward you. You don't believe it will ever
        reach the ground.

Wood Ibis

Here they come to dance the mud
    from the shallows of the oxbow lake.
The sky is undone and shattered
    into hundreds of them. With their bald heads
and wrinkled necks they must be old men.
    Conjuring fish and frogs and water snakes,
summoning each as prophecy and occultation.

The evening his wife died he stood
    on the back porch and heard them bellowing:
what arises from the lungs is hollowness
    itself, forced air compressed as though to stone.
The white of the birds devours
    the surface of the lake: what else can it do?

In the ancient covenant the hours are churned
    as rising silt. He sees it sometimes
as a dream: the great birds lifting themselves

back into the sky, the black wingtips
stirring the low slung clouds.

Bottomlands Inheritance

He sat on the back porch.
Chorus frogs from the cypress swamp
carried in their voices
the fetid smells of muck
congealing on the surface
of the shallow waters. Sometimes a white ibis
flew up from the black willows
and made of its wings an occultation.
His grandmother knew to grind
up pickerelweeds, epidendrums,
and damselflies to make a potion.
He knew to listen in his dreams
to the alligator snapping turtle
rising from the brackish waters,
to the moon-white mouth
of the water moccasin opening
as the first syllable. When his wife
died a piercing scream from a bobcat
lifted from beyond the black tupelos,
and in the morning a dense mist
rose from the oxbow lake
as though to smother him.
As a child he would tremble if he saw
a barred owl sitting on a possumhaw limb
in bright daylight, and he would walk
around and around the tree, hoping
the bird would swivel and swivel
its neck until it snapped. Now he sat
on the back porch and gazed out
at the provenance of Spanish moss
and duckweed. Something was watching
from the sweetgum trees. He knew
it was the owlit always was.
And always it was eyeing him.

A cappella

Had I lost you as a girl,
kitten purrs and blushing giggles,
I would have hidden beneath the front porch,
knelt in the sand, been your loyal mangy pet,
watching for the sight of your boots on the stairs.

Had I lost you as your bride,
still innocent and dressed in lace,
I would have tossed my veil into the sea
and followed it to a watery grave,
been your sacrifice, your Juliet, your Ophelia.

Had I lost you as the mother of your child,
my milk would have grown sour,
the cradle been still , and our infant's cries
would have drowned in the deluge
of tears pouring from my selfish eyes.

Had I lost you as an old woman,
leaning on you for each step,
relying on your sense of direction
to help me find my way home,
I would have wandered into traffic,
or been swept beneath the bridge, homeless.

I lost you in my prime, when dreams of being a mother
had faded, when my legs had grown strong enough
to stand alone, when I could see myself beyond
a vessel or a womb, when my voice was full and clear,
able to carry our song a cappella with perfect timing.

Lunch Break

I am liking it here these weeks,
this conjunction,
this pedestrian plaza, these towers,
the nooncrowd, anonymous community,
my deli sandwich, my share of bench.

And through there, up there,
on the eave of the cathedral,
perches the gargoyle.

Because also here, one day lately,
two surveyors were unaccountably at work
with their tripod, scope, and sighting pole.

I took them and their intent
for my fantasy.
Of impassioned geometricians
gridding the landscape in three dimensions
with beams of figmentation,
unobstructed by geology or architecture,
undeterred by utility,
projection for projection's sake,
marvelous, pure, exquisitely ordered.

Under the purview here of the gargoyle,
impassioned nihilist,
maliciously disengaged.

I am liking it here,
this defining space,
plaza, nooncrowd,
brightly urban,
deli sandwich, share of bench.

graveyard

maimed, crippled poems lie in the dark
behind bookshelves or crushed beneath
the shuffling tread of days

I remember wrapping the bones
with pieces of flesh peeled and ragged
still incomplete

the stench of the dead
must be covered up, hidden, buried
under cracks in the surface

ghosts rise at midnight some nights
my scars start to itch, voices whisper
I will come undone

Marquette Branch, Oct. 26, 2009

First, I tell them to not write the obvious.
Don't say that they're prisoners.
Show that they're prisoners.
Ban the word "prison," I say.
They don't know what this room looks like.
They don't know there's no bars in the entire place.

You see this fly strip,
it looks like it hasn't been changed
in eight years.
"Seventeen," Troy says.
"How do you know seventeen?"
"Because I been here that long, and it's never been changed."

So paint that for them.
You see all these flies,
you see how this fly has been rotting for eighteen years,
describe it.
You see how hard that fly is,
like a little rock.

"That's us," Troy says.
"What?"
"We're those flies."
Right, I say,
exactly,
if you understand that, you understand poetry.

I Don't Have a Response for That

I'm here to help, I say
I know what it was like for you guys,
kind of,

when I was in Desert Storm
they cut off all forms of communication.
We couldn't make calls.
Nothing, except for letters.
And that's what it is for most of you.

So I wanna teach you how to communicate
with your family.

"What if you killed everyone in your family?"

Middle Age

There are no city-chewed streets,
only white and lilac blooming dogwood trees.
Cars with whisper engines
sweep past.

It is spring, not mid-winter,
already my light coat is a burden.
It is true, at every early-morning,
still dark, or pale-shadowed corner,

I meet my father, too.
My age, he is dead,
stares as blindly
as in life.

Why ask him to be forgiven
when I know not who I hurt?
I injure only the living.
He tracks my every step.

He is what has passed, while I wait
to be spirited.
Tonight,
I lay my head down with the dead.

Explaining the Wound

–for Dick Allen

We sit across a lunch of corn dogs and roast beef,
when my friend catches me short
by asking to see my wound.
I look at my blood-free palms
and pull up my shirt
thinking there's a forgotten scar
or some stigmata somewhere, but no
I've never had any surgery done on me
other than a late circumcision
or the extraction of a tooth.
Soon enough he tells me
he's thinking of Malcolm Cowley's essay
on what makes writers write—
some childhood trauma
ensiloed in the brain,
like boiled cotton or unsold grain.
Given this clue, I spend a few minutes
trying to fit an answer to his question;
pick one, I say, my bout with polio,
the loss of cousins and aunts in Brataslava
and Hungary during the war,
a cafeteria of disappointments.
But nothing in my history
really convinces him or me, any more
than Cowley's theory consoles us for the mystery
of why we live to die.
Done with our cokes, I rise to tell him goodbye,
sly in my addiction to facts,
and thank him for his company.
All he does is smile his Buddhist smile—
me not knowing why.

The Girl in Section 342

One row down at Oriole Park
and just to the right of me,
the same girl returns in the same uniform:
rimless glasses and a gingham dress,
its left sleeve pinned back, empty.
I don't know and am afraid to ask
how much they took off and why.
Was it a tumor in the humerus
or a trolley that dragged her along
and wouldn't stop,
or an accident at the butcher shop
or a car wreck?
Was it a gunshot wound and
suppuration in her veins that crept
up and almost engulfed her?
Who can guess?
I watch her nimbly climb the steps
to her seat, a cardboard tray with nachos
and a cola balanced in the one good hand.
My male mind wonders how she can
apply mascara at the start of the day
and what she does when her bra slips off?
I'd like to know how she holds a child
or strokes a lover and if he dares to touch
her camouflaged stump with a thrill
or does fear prick at his fingertips?
I notice she never comes alone
and it's often not the same man;
but why do I care?
When the next batter swings, I turn away,
having better things to do than stare
at a dismemberment like mine.

Turner Sets Out in a Snowstorm

Wishing to paint a steamboat in a snowstorm
Turner, in his last decade
had himself strapped to the *Ariel's* swinging mast

for four hours. He was only five foot three
but held to this perch by bitter rope,
stood like a great unblinking owl
and dreamed of a locomotive throwing off steam
while smoke and spray billowed and foamed
across the decks and almost swept him clear.
All the while, his frozen gaze tongued the napes
of boarding waves like maidens' necks, while bits
of salt clotted the sheets and his rime-hung
lashes. When the white caps at last whipped off
the wave tops, wind frothed the air he breathed in
and the lung of the storm gagged him;
it turned the ocean to steam and stung his brow
with diamond-shaped ice drops.
Was all this pain endured just to paint a souvenir
of the real? In Turner's illusion the ship slides down
a red and yellow maelstrom and hurtles itself at us,
at him, a churning engine slipping its watery tracks.

What the Bay Provides

At Norfolk, the well-sounded and restless sea
spills into the Bay and rushes to meet rivers flooding
to the east, west and north of the ocean's mouth, the chill
water carrying its cargo of crab, sook and spat, down below
the warm riverine current. To grow, to meet, to mate
to feed the world along the banks of its watery ballroom,
to be caught in pots and trotlines, seduced by chicken necks
and doors that snap shut just behind cone-shaped tunnels
and fate. Hauled up in flat-bottomed boats, trimmed fair
and transported to the fisher-houses of Smith and Tangier islands,
peeling and soft in old wooden floats, skinned by women
who speak with an Elizabethan "r", they make
one last watery trip across Tangier Sound to the plants
in Crisfield, where life and its shell are made soft and delicate,
eaten moist on the tongue with a briny smell
that the nose recalls each time it drowns below the horizon of air.

Not Bringing Souvenirs

Although she remains
as a small changing wavelet
through which the particles pass,

everything around her
flows away, all the
material nuggets.

I can't bring
tokens of a home
she can't connect again.

Even the molecules of
her lifetime
scatter.

A Compendium of Daydreams

I forget where I
left the car, and forget
where I live.
I run crazy through the streets
while time slides away on greased rails.
Those who miss me
wait.

A party forces my choices.
I grin for some of them
and leave the rest in the cold.
They wait for me, not present to see,
not knowing I am gone.

We emerge from the battle,
my friends
seeping away into the ground.
I am joyous
even while they
say farewell to the grass.

Early Lessons

Bum-banging satchel belaboured me
running the long street to school.

The mason, hand bunched thick
round the stock of a flat chisel,
watched me through glasses
frosted by a million flying shards,
returned to peck at that day's shape.
Strange curves emerged
from a peck, peck, pecking,
patient as dripping water,
that discovered bits of houses
in the bones of earth.

The oily shed, home to an old tank engine
that seethed like a great black kettle on a hob
steam flowered from sprung seams.
I knew the sear of that coal-gulping maw
and the sudden vent of dragon breath
that filled the yard with scalding vapours
and belches of sulphur that engorged a sky
bannered with the smoke of a town girded for war.

In the farrier's hearth,
a hoop glowed in its golden nest of coke
bellowed to a heat I felt feet away.
Mightily rang the anvil with his bouncing hammer,
as he fettled the sparking iron, plunged it back
into the belly of fire. Swarthy and grimed,
he chimed from the heart of a Vulcan reek
of quenched iron and burnt hoof.

Late as usual, I left to chase
into the place of hard desks
chalk and the long slow plod of hours;
a place where good French seemed a logical impossibility
and geometry was a foreign language.

Requiem: Spring 1943

Chattering with excitement we traipsed
up from the clamour of mills
to the deep woods, loud with Spring.   .

Lads! Raucous, war-lean,
muscled like skinned rabbits
daft as otters, dared the chill of the cut.

Spencer took me deeper.

The air rifle, hung broken over his arm,
slim levers and hinges relaxed,
sleek and well-oiled; pellets in his mouth.

Deeper he took me

to the bosky, brambled heart.
Spring shot lank swift life.
Gas-flamed leaves flared green

In sunlight leaking through a thin canopy,
a sudden thrill of song burst from a twig,
where a yellow hammer sang.

Levers and hinges slid and closed.
Bright feathers bloomed and spun
in the shattered Eden-light,

the unravelled bird bounced upon leaf-mould.
Spencer, his face mottled with triumph;
stole away looking for other things to kill.

The trees were stunned, shade
of unfolding leaf, as I trod a soft path
where the slow waters oozed.

A gaped and silenced beak
tipped with a bead of bright blood.

Appellation

CLAREMONT, CALIFORNIA—

A college classmate called out, "Hey, Solomon—you make it home for the holidays this weekend?"

Confused, I replied, "What holidays? I've been here all weekend."

Stunned, he stammered, "What? You're not Jewish?"

Now it was my turn to be stunned. I'd never thought about it. "No," I confessed.

He fixed his eyes on mine, and said, "With a name like Solomon, and a nose like that, you look like you come right off the streets of New York."

It was the last I ever heard from him.

HAIFA, ISRAEL—

Palmach squad leader turned irrigation engineer, David Karmeli told me how he'd taken his name [which means *my Carmel* in Hebrew] from the Mount on which his adopted city grew. Our conversation wound around, late into the night.

At one point he asked me, "Are you Jewish?"

I told him, "I don't know."

"What a strange answer," he said.

"By religion? No. But by heritage? We just don't know."

I explained, according to our family story: "My great-grandfather was found a young orphan, wandering along the Oklahoma trail. He knew little of his past and was raised by the family that found him. He later became a circuit-riding Baptist preacher in the Oklahoma Territory. But we know nothing of what came before."

"Ah," Karmeli sighed, "another soul lost to us."

WESTMINSTER, COLORADO—

Lawrence Dooley, a Syrian colleague, seemed agitated and ill at ease, but I didn't know why.

"Are you sure," he asked me, "that you're the best one to be going to Saudi Arabia? I know you'd do a great job for us there, but Dale could handle all that, and we could really use you on the Venezuela project instead."

He couldn't help kissin' up. It was his nature. Still, it was irritating. And I knew he didn't care about the Venezuela job—it was out of his territory.

But I didn't get what he was driving at, at least not at first.

Dooley kept dropping his less-than-subtle hints.

"If Dale went to Saudi, he could meet with Sabour in Cairo on the way back."

At last I figured it out, but went ahead with my plans for the trip anyway. I wanted to see the Saudi-Shirock job site first hand.

Finally, Dooley came into my office and closed the door behind him. His look was more than serious.

"You know"—he paused for effect—"in some parts of the world it may not always be safe for someone with a name like Solomon."

CAIRO, EGYPT—

Four of us had been selected for the technical exchange with Egypt. We were to spend a week in Cairo discussing the latest advances in irrigation and water management with experts from the Egyptian Society of Agricultural Engineers.

The host delegation met us at the airport in Heliopolis, and everyone introduced themselves. As it happened, my Egyptian counterpart was named Dr. Suleiman.

As he greeted me, he grinned and remarked heartily "Ah, Solomon—a good Arabic name!"

DZHAMBUL, KAZAKHSTAN, USSR—

Fresno and Dzhambul had recently been paired as sister-cities. City in Russian is a masculine noun, so as ceremonial jokes would later point out endlessly, we became all combinations of sister- and brother-cities.

Exchange visits were hurriedly arranged, and I joined the first group from Fresno State University to visit the Dzhambul Irrigation, Land Reclamation and Civil Engineering Institute. As Galiya, our translator, introduced everyone, I found myself face to face with Vice-Rector Zhusup Suleimenov. We shook hands, and he spoke:

"Mozhet Bwet—

"Perhaps," he said, "you and I are brothers."

What We're Spared

for Kevin R. Wood

Yes, of course! This is
what it feels like—
I'd seen it on TV shows
like *ER* and *Strong Medicine*:
those countless dead as they gasp
out their last breath, just as
they settle into the stillness
which looks very much like sleep.
I watched it with the indifference
of one who presumes immunity
from such pain, cut off,
as if viewing it through a window.
Only now the beep of your heart monitor
surrounds me, the smell of death
stings my nose, and I feel your skin
grow cold as I grasp your toes.
This is what we're spared
through the glass tubes as we watch
numb in our living rooms. This,
and the emptiness that makes you
feel just as much a corpse.

When Your World Tilts

for Kevin

nothing is upside down
like one would expect things
to be. The moon still pursues
our sun across the sky
as if it were a criminal
it can never apprehend. Darkness
remains hitched to it, a banner of night
is dragged over the Earth.

You go out for an evening

walk, and confused birds sing
in their usual way to a dawn which doesn't arrive. Alive,
you strut like the pedestrians
your heels rap past along the way—
they do not suspect a thing,
to them you are everyone else.
Only you feel the disease eat
at you; that piranha which consumes you
inside, only you can see the HIV
while it gradually siphons your life.

The Last Time

for Kevin

The last time we laid together
tangled in our sheets, his head turned

and I looked through the darkness
into his eyes. His black sockets

searched mine, and the world
seemed to slow to a stillness

in which his rattled breaths were the only sound.
His sweat-chilled hand gripped mine

as he spoke what I'd known for a week:
soon I'll drift off to sleep, I won't wake up

again. Then his choked snores echoed
through the room like damnation,

the music of death I'd learned to doze to
when I'd nod off and live his end once more.

Contracting

for Kevin R. Wood

He raises his arms
in the shadows of his bedroom
like charcoal colored wings;
an Angel of death arched
above me—how I burn
for him to love me. Outside,
a Florida thunderstorm bucks the oaks
the way his body heaves
against mine, it's divine
how he sacrifices me
on the altar of his bed. Tonight,
death tastes like the Colgate
he brushes against my lips,
feels like the way he spears me
with each thrust of his hips, it runs
off his skin warm as blood.
Lord, the thrust of his rod stabs me
deep, the virus that spills out
will one day lull me to sleep.

It's Bound to Happen

The dog will leap her fence, chase a liberty
that zags like a startled rabbit under the skirts
of evergreens. Open windows will invite rain.
Water stains will blossom on the ceiling tiles,
expand above our heads like tarnished halos.

The birdhouse's soft wood will absorb too
much afternoon, vex the string that bears
its weight. Eggs will crack, abort their hearts.
Sparrows will seek new twig and string.
I'll forget my name, misplace my voice's tenor.

Your hair will silver—mine will thin.
On a Sunday morning, you'll drape my lap
with blue quilt, wheel me beneath the dogwood—
its pink petals slapping the hour like confetti.
You'll hum a song and I'll remember it.

Itinerary

Today, I'd like to visit a small book shop.
Its floors should creek beneath my meander—
Auden to Whitman. Steep stairs lead to second floor
shadows and open windows invite scents

of soft rain. Of course, it's still morning—
a coffee pot snores on the counter.
Stacks of Styrofoam cups ring its pop
and gurgle like the circumference of Stonehenge.

In a brittle chair, I'll share a cookie with Milton,
a fallen angel, a savior who redeemed us all.
Outside, tulips, laden with mist, will bow bright
heads to pray. A man, wrinkled, whiskered white,

will step into the shop—shelter from a maturing
wind. He'll trod through an hour behind a hot tea's
steam, quietly talking with Wordsworth's lonely cloud.
I'll offer him my chair and we'll be friends.

Alternative Yuletide

No, this isn't what you think.
This won't be a poem for Jews for Jesus.

There won't be a dilution of symbols here,
nor a call to theological potpourri.

No, this won't be a Irving Berlin-ish revelrie,
sparkling in sleigh bells and whiteness.

Instead, there will be gratitude for the day off,
for the streets so desolate, for the stores sealed,

There will be relief in freedom from obligation and the search for objects.
There will be contentment in apart-ness, in not looking in from the out-
    side.

We will meet beneath the cinema's neon rimmed crystal chandelier,
consider the various offerings, without hurry, and despite the queues,
    without stress.

Afterwards, we will trek downtown, no matter the weather,
where avenues narrow to alleys, where restaurant windows perspire in
    beckoning.

There we will discuss what we've seen,
savor the vigorous fare, envisioned across oceans, revised here.

We will toast this plenty—the fellowship,
the nourishment, the possibilities for renewal,

this mild delight, this muted reverence,
this holiday.

Idyll

Cherish this banality, my love—
the day unfurling into splendor.
Coffee drifts from below into our reading lairs;
a lawn mower hums in the distance,
earth and words intoxicating us from dream.

Your footsteps patter down the corridor;
your night clothes gleam where the sun does not pierce,
a vision so fleeting yet glimpsed these countless times.
Today I won't rise to catch it.
I'll know you're there simply by the measure of my reverie,
carved in calm,
unmoved by the neighbor dog's yapping.
The weekend section spreads amply around the dining room table,
marked by circles of varying urgency.
Perhaps we will forage for treasure abandoned;
perhaps we will sample the fruit of vineyards coaxed into perfection.
Before we go to wherever we go,
I want to lift your hair, nuzzle your nape,
whisper my tender grateful nothings:
whatever these hours shall hold,
this is good, this is plenty.

Islands

He bought a doll-size version of his own house,
had it custom-built according to his measurements,
his meticulous observations. Then he set about
its decoration—the colour of the walls,

carpet patterns, kitchen fittings, furniture,
bathroom suite. On tables, he put tiny cups and saucers,
carefully chosen; cut clothes from fabrics tracked down
over time, and hung them in the wardrobes,

always slightly open, as if just lately left that way.
He wired it up from ground floor to the attic, so that
wall lights and table lamps all worked:
adjusted through the day, turned off at night.

Coloured cellophane warmed the fireplace,
a small receiver played Radio Four.
Beside a baby baby-grand piano, he placed
a music stand; from time to time he'd turn the pages.

He kept it covered over, in a shed they never visited.
If they'd seen it, they'd have recognised
their house but they'd have understood
from every detail, that this was not their home.

In Step

Run with me
summer night

endless alleyway
a thousand backyards

passing porchlights
sillouttes in windows

rhythm of feet
gravel and asphalt

stars shaking like salt
tasting their eternity

breathing
halo of earth.

Birdwatcher

For seven years I've tried to approach the ground zero
of my neighborhood, which happens to be the nation's,
my daily walk to work, for a long time, through allies
of wreckage, detours that couldn't circle wider
than the stench of burning flesh, and though
the rubble was carried off and quotidian alarms
sounded the all-clear, the horns triggering explosives
to sink new foundations, the dwelling of our
persistent belief in a future, and my own, the ribs
of the new station arcing like a nest, I wake to a life
still at the edge of ruins, a train snaking round the pit
to disgorge its passengers onto a platform, its length
overlapped in the fog of histories, like the long approach
to Athena's throne, or the Via Appia, but paved over,
stairs at the end rising to the fences, which lead me
round the rim, walking into the low, autumn sun
pressing metallic foil to the bell towers of St. Paul's
and Trinity Church, slowly lifting its head above rooftops,
stretching its fingers through streets, poking the Hudson,
seeming to search with a birdwatcher's quiet caution
for a glimpse of the shadows it can cast but never catch.

Secret Door

I looked down an alley between houses
that seemed to stretch the day's residual light
to the rooftops, compacting distant bridges,
traffic, power lines and towers into its narrow
six-foot passage between bricks and siding.
It was a three-story keyhole into a room reserved
only for trolls and angels, a mythical insight
into forces flying among the sliding headlights
that slowly blinked on along the interstate,
the vague flapping of birds going gray
and mysterious in the thickening dark, steam
and exhaust fumes throwing curtains back
in perpetual disclosure, up the horizon line
stretched like the world's windowsill, the ledge

spilling onto landscapes which, although
visible to no one, are seeded by the bare trees
rooted in this foreground, in this neighbor's yard
dense with lean endurances and knuckled bark,
of naked maples and mulberries still shedding,
and that will continue to shed all winter long
a meaning free of every burden and reason.

Ode to a Cigarette Lighter

A silver cap, a flint,
the mechanism
for flame to dance,
your orange the pits of hell,
your yellow
the voice of longing.

You are but a simple thing,
a shape friendly to touch
a smooth fit for the palm
that desires none other
than to set you free.

With flicks and sparks
you aim for stardom,
the cigarette coughs into being
your life, suddenly extinguished
as your breath settles
into a gaseous blue canister.

Into a netherworld
of pressed cotton, lint
the warmth shared,
you await the next deciding moment
when kindling is sought,

the smell of your passing,
your after affects,
as lungs claw for breath,
a hand deftly turning you—
over and over.

Dream Animals: Regretasaurus

This is a creature best kept at bay.
They come in all sizes, shapes and colors.
Some of them have wings, almost all
of them have a bite worse than a viper's.

Regretasaurus is like a vapor. It can
breeze its way into our lungs with the wind.
Once in, it heads for the mind and attaches
itself—a leech feasting on strange things.

It will spend as much time contemplating
the coupon one forgot to use at the market
as the last words one never got the chance
to say to a dying loved one or friend.

One or two of these should drive a man
insane. But the fact is that we play host
to hordes of them as if our brains were hives
and they the workers, drones, and queen bees.

By the time we are old, they're the only friends
worth having. All the *what ifs and I should'ves*
pile up like logs in a beaver dam until a pool
of regret, repentance and repetition appears.

In the end, it floods everything. It is from
this pool we must fish out our supper,
wash our dirty linens, quench our thirst,
baptize our lives and make our bitter teas.

Music for the Parade

He was not so much a witness
as an observer of his life.
He knew no prayers that might
sweeten the darkness,
no litany of sacred words
that could soothe his little fears.

One never really held conversations

with him—one was talked to,
informed, chided, and dismissed.
It wasn't that he couldn't listen,
it was more likely he was too busy
preparing his comeback to hear.

And there was the problem with music.
He knew nothing about it but what
he liked and didn't. He needed nothing
more and never went calling unless
he brought with him the music to be
listened to during his little parade.

He collected opinions like other people
collect string and knew more about
gates than anyone I've ever met. He
knew how to keep them closed. These
included the gates to heart, his home,
and whatever gardens he tried to grow.

Translations

Bertolt Brecht (1898–1956) obtained fame as a playwright and theatrical innovator while spending most of his life in and out of exile for his political beliefs. He was a committed Marxist and in February 1933 left Germany due to his anti-Nazi political beliefs for numerous locations in Europe while he awaited a US visa. In exile he complete plays such as *Mother Courage and her Children, The Good Person of Szechwan*, and *The Resistible Rise of Arturo Uri*, a thinly disguised parady of Hitler. In 1941 he came to the US, attempting to become a Hollywood screen writer. In 1947, during the years of the "red scare," the House Un-American Activities Committee called the playwright to account for his communist activities. While he outwitted his interrogators, Brecht feared the political climate in the US and caught a plane to Switzerland after his testimony. On October 22, 1948, after 15 years of exile, Bertolt Brecht returned to Germany, settling in East Berlin where he was welcomed by the Communist cultural establishment. Brecht will be forever enshrined in popular culture as the lyricist of the song "Mack the Knife" from his play *The Threepenny Opera*.

Of Poor B. B.

I, Bertolt Brecht, came out of the black forests.
My mother carried me into the cities while I lay
Inside her body. And the chill of the forests
Will remain inside me until my dying day.

In the asphalt city I'm at home. From the beginning
Provided with every last sacrament:
With newspapers. And tobacco. And brandy.
To the end distrustful, lazy, and content.

I am friendly to people. I put on
A stiff hat according to their custom.
I say: They're animals with quite a peculiar smell.
And I say: What does it matter, I am too.

Occasionally in the morning I sit

A woman or two on my empty rocking chairs
And gaze at them thoughtlessly and say:
In me you have someone who can't be trusted.

Toward evening, I gather men around me,
We address one another as "gentlemen."
They rest their feet on my tabletops
And say: Things will get better for us, and I don't ask when.

Toward morning in the grey light the fir trees piss
And their vermin, the birds, begin to chirp.
At that hour I drain my glass in town and chuck
The cigar butt and worriedly fall asleep.

We have sat, an easy generation,
In houses thought to be indestructible
(So we have built those tall boxes on the island of Manhattan
And those thin antennae that amuse the Atlantic swell).

All that will remain of these cities is the wind that passed through them!
The house makes the consumer happy: he empties it out.
We know that we are only tenants, provisional ones,
And after us there'll be nothing much worth talking about.

In the earthquakes to come, I very much hope
I don't let my cigar go out, embittered or not,
I, Bertolt Brecht, carried into the asphalt cities
From the black forests inside my mother long ago.

Return

Hometown, how will it look then?
Following swarms of bombers
I have come home.
But where is it? Where the towering
Mountains of smoke rise.
There in the flames,
It's there.

Hometown, how will it receive me then?
Before me the bombers come. Deadly swarms
Announce my return. Raging fires

Precede the homecoming son.

Thoughts on the Length of Exile

I.

Don't hammer any nails into the wall.
Throw your coat across the chair.
Why plan for four days?
Tomorrow you'll be heading home.

Leave the little tree unwatered.
Why ever plant a tree?
Before it grows high as a doorstep
you'll pack your bags and be gone from here.

Pull your cap down over your eyes when people pass!
What's the use of thumbing through a foreign grammar.
The message that will call you home
is written in a language you already know.

Just as the plaster peels from the ceiling
(Don't worry about the repairs!),
The block of force will crumble
That has been set up at the border
To keep out justice.

II.

See that nail you hammered into the wall.
When do you think you'll return?
Do you want to know what you believe in your heart?

Day after day
You work for liberation.
You sit in your room writing.
Do you want to know how you really feel about your work?
See that little chestnut tree in the corner of the yard,
You just carried it a canfull of water!

To Those Who Come After

I.

Truly I live in a bleak age.
The innocent word is foolish. A smooth brow
Is a sign of insensitivity. The laughing man
Has to receive
The dreadful news.

What times are these when
A conversation about trees is almost a crime
Because it contains a silence about so many atrocities.
That man there calmly crossing the streets,
Hasn't he stopped being reachable
For his friends in need?

True, I still earn my living
But, believe me, it's only through luck. Nothing
I do gives me the right to eat my fill.
Only by chance have I been spared. (If my luck gives out I'll be lost).

They tell me: eat and drink. Be happy that you can.
But how can I eat and drink when
I snatch what I eat from the hungry man, and
My glass of water deprives the man dying of thirst.
And yet I eat and drink

I wish I were also wise.
In the old books it says what it means to be wise:
Stay away from the strife of the world and spend
Your short time without fear,
Refrain from violence,
Return good for evil,
Don't fulfill your desires, but forget them instead,
and you'll be wise.
Everything that I can not do:
Truly I live in a bleak age.

II.

I came to the cities in a time of disorder
When hunger ran rampant.
I joined with the people in a time of rebellion
And revolted as they did.
So passed the time

Granted me on earth.

I ate my meals between battles.
I slept beside murderers.
Heedlessly I pursued love
And looked on nature without patience.
So passed the time
Granted me on earth.

In my time the streets led into quagmires.
Speech betrayed me to the butcher.
There was little I could do. But I hoped
The rulers sat less secure because of me.
So passed the time
Granted me on earth.

My strength was small. The goal
Lay far ahead.
It was clearly visible, even
If for me hard to reach.
So passed the time
Granted me on earth.

III.

You who will emerge out of this deluge
We drown in,
Remember
When you speak of our weaknesses
About the bleak age
You escaped.

We went forth, changing countries more often than shoes
Through the wars of the classes, despairing
When there was only injustice and no rebellion.

Yet because of this we know:
Even hatred of meanness
Distorts a man's features.
Even anger over injustice
Makes his voice hoarse. Ah, we
Who wanted to prepare the ground for kindness
Couldn't be kind to ourselves.

But you, if it ever happens

That men become the helpers of men,
Remember us
With a little indulgence.

translated from the German by Jim Doss

Ernest Bryll, born in 1935 in Warsaw, Poland, is a very popular poet, writer, lyricist, journalist, translator (from Irish, Czech and Yiddish), film critic, and diplomat. Among his foreign country postings is a 1991–1995 ambassadorship to the Irish Republic. He is an author of some fifty volumes of poetry, plays, and prose, and a co-translator of seven books on Irish literature. Some of his plays have attained record popularity with audiences, such as *Painted on Glass*, which has been performed on stage in Bratislava, Slovakia, continuously since 1974. His poems have been adapted as lyrics for hit songs by some of the best Polish singers.

Nearby, nearby it is hardest to hear. . .

Nearby, nearby it is hardest to hear
If the leaf talks to us. If the angel has tripped
And gotten soiled in the dirty puddle that
Remains forever on the road ahead.

From nearby it is the longest path to travel
To hear something, someone's call for help.
Too close the cry. Not audible so near.
Too close, it stinks. No room to breathe.

Oh, it's better from afar. First, we catch our breaths
Then we compose long letters
To the angel. Let him come to the one who calls
Apparently for help. The angel knows
For he looks from above.

Let's not doubt
The ones from afar are nearby.

The Lamb

The lamb on brittle legs
Stood in a faded meadow. Waiting
He might live or be dead
—All in the man's hands

And the hands squeezed the air
Trembling to the very horizon
And a dirty finger covered
Even parts of heaven
We little people lost on the journey
—And what could we have done?
—What could we have used to stop
The giant's ruthless hands?
And yet so many ran
Toward the darkness—As into flames
The army of paupers
Fought for the innocent lamb

✳ ✳ ✳ ✳

To fall asleep in eternity's palm—in peace
As if its fingers were never
To close, to clench, to lock
Around you
Into a fist smaller than a day, a moment
A second... A grave

✳ ✳ ✳ ✳

In the gale like a river thickening above
We heard your breath—oh, angry God

And rather than fall, perish in the flood
We nailed together our fragile boats

And rather than like wax in the Lord's hand melting
We chose the art of sailing

The One Who

The one who harmed a simple man
Will find verse-makers who will erase all
And a historian deft with arguments
Who will sculpt the events with such a noble face
As events have never worn before
The one who perpetrated harm—if he gets through
Will find his own justice in the ages' darkness
Though he sowed storms he will have a sweet harvest

Such is the experience. And we would want
The words of a poet to be feared
The emperors to sweat in their crumpled sheets
Thinking what has been written about them

Such is the experience, always known
And always the stupid poets run against it

translated from the Polish by Danuta E. Kosk-Kosicka

Ebba Lindqvist (1908–1995) was a Swedish poet who, despite personal hardships and a nomadic life, published all fourteen of her collections at Sweden's leading publishing house, Bonniers. Ebba Lindqvist lived in Paris, Berlin, New York, Nairobi, Leipzig, Beirut, Alicante and several Swedish locations. At various times in her life, she was caretaker for family members who were seriously disabled, including her mother, her husband, and two of her three children. She studied at Uppsala University and Columbia University, and was fluent in many languages. Her poems seem simple, but are full of nuances. Although over one hundred of her poems have been set to music, these two poems, approved by her estate, are the first of her work to be published in English.

What the Preacher Saw

This is what the Preacher saw.
All this beauty.
Trees filtering the sunlight.
The vapor in a red tremble
on the kiln-like mountain.
This earth that bounteously
brings forth fruit.
This is what the Preacher saw,
and he understood:
all the rest is vanity.
And all he asked for,
and all he wished his fellow man,
was a handful of tranquility.

Monologue in Hades

(Eurydice to Orpheus)

Who said I was willing to go with you, Orpheus?
Why were you so certain, that you came to find me?
To force me back, step by step?
Once our love was lovely, and never shall it be said otherwise.
But life does not tempt me now. Even up there
in the land of sunlight, cold shadows
will come creeping across the mountain. I know. I remember.
No one felt the coldness of your heart as I did.
The sun has dark spots. Eros has dark wings.
And in the darkness of night I heard, even while on earth,
the barking of the hounds of Hell.—Don't think I grieve
because you failed, because you turned around to look. Oh, no one
knows your failings as I do. Worn out, you came back,
always came back to me, after the feasts and triumphal processions,
dropped your lyre on the ground, fell into my arms to forget
the bacchantes, the songs, the wine. I, your faithful love, who waited
     alone.
No songs for me. Never a joy ride in the sunshine.
Never the airy flight of birds. Orpheus came home just too tired.
Don't think that I grieve. I chose a life in Hades.
It was not the viper that chose me. It was I who chose the viper.
I spied it in the meadow among the flowers. I wanted the poison.
I never existed until I came here, to the realm of shadows
Life shoves us up against the wall. Life demands an answer.
Life has words sharp as spears that pierce the heart.
The blood drops so quietly, so quietly, and no one sees how it drops.
And yet—again and again I repeat it, Orpheus:
Once our love was lovely, and never shall it be said otherwise.
But it was not love I followed. Trembling and pale,
staggering and weary, I followed the lyre and the song.
The song about the sun and the winds. The song about the sea and its
     waves.
The song of the comeliness of earth, when the poppy opens in spring.
The song about everything the earth gives, but even more
about that it does not give. About something greater than life,
about something greater than the human heart and greater than love.
The song about something more lovely than life.
The song that is greater than love or death.

The song that is greater than song. Oh, all things on earth
will crumble to dust;
I will forget it all, but never the song.
Once, only once, did you play your song for me.
Only once—in the chilling realm of shadows.
Once I had a life on earth. On earth, oh,
I yield it gladly to those strong enough to live. But
who said I was willing to go with you, Orpheus?
Life does not tempt me now.
I have no longing to return.

Translated from the Swedish by Janice D. Soderling

Al Mahmud (1936–) is one of Bangladesh's leading Bengali poets. His first collection of poem *Lok Lokantor* (*People and Places*) was published in 1963. Later books, such as *Sonali Kabin* (*The Golden Wedding Document*; 1966) consolidated his reputation. In addition to writing poetry, Mahmud writes short stories, novels and essays among which *Pankourir Rakta* (*The Cormorant's Blood*) is considered to be the most famous.

The Cormorant's Blood

I did not notice the black bird at first. I was intently looking at a big white heron, gaily bending its neck, ready to peck into the clear water. My steps were light, I knew I would be able to knock that strange bird over from a great distance; there was another reason for not hurrying too much: birds like emerald dove or pygmy-geese, a great find for any hunter, were hard to come by in this area. Strewn all over the field were a few ashen-black and white cranes and a flock of mynahs. The latter were fluttering over the swamp; whenever I walked past them they squeaked and moved away; the noise was a pain, how Jibanananda Das wrote poems about these blighted creatures I never understood. Softly holding the gun in my left hand I carefully crossed the field and stepped into the bog; even though there was a pothole or two filled with water, the swamp was dry. As it was the middle of winter, the swamp had dried, becoming soft and heavy like the hide of wild swine. In the last few days a tuft of grass grew on the dried mud; from a distance it looked like a bed of some strange heavy-petalled flower. This kind of grass did not cluster around each other much, thank god for that. And because of this, because the grass did not come out in a bunch, the bog, though it looked like a mass of green at the beginning, later, as I got closer, resembled more and more a bush of some unknown wild flower, floating in a wave of soft wet earth.

Casting a sharp quick glance at the white heron I got down to the marsh. Though my trousers were rolled up to the knee, perhaps because I was extremely cautious, only my ankles plunged into the mud, where I dragged myself. The bird could be seen clearly now; I looked for the right place to ready myself and shoot.

Before me, on a big blade of grass, was a wide-petalled flower. It should not be bad to stand there to shoot; careful so as not to stamp the petals, I stood on the ground barefooted and widened my legs. As I did so the grass under my feet flattened; it would have been better if I could widen my legs more, then I would have been able to hold the gun properly. But the patch of grass here was too small to do that. I looked around myself: at my back, about a quarter of a mile away was my father-in-law's house, the great mango tree beside it and at the front, in the yard, amidst a stack of hay two calves were chewing. When I was leaving the house with the gun, my wife Adina said, "You have to bring me a hornbill's beak, I will wait for you here under this tree."

"Please do. Why only a hornbill's beak? If you wish, I can bring the air's feather for you."

Hiding her face with the corner of her sari Adina started laughing, and in that bout of mirth and happiness her back bent, then she stole quick glances around, careful not to attract the attention of the elders. We had got married seven days ago, and still Adina thought it would be a matter of shame if our elders found us flirting. But Adina was not really from the country, her parents had settled in Comilla town, their house was beside ours; for the last fifteen years we had been neighbours. Her father was the Third Supervisor at the Gomati Dam project; a hard-working family, with five children. Adina's two brothers ran a shop that dealt in, with great difficulty, spare parts of motorcycles and bi-cycles and tri-shaws. Her two sisters went to school, and Adina had just enrolled into the college after passing her entrance exams. After that, after she entered the college, we got married; she became my wife.

I noticed that she was not standing at the foot of the tree for the hornbill's beak. Turning round, I looked at the heron, which, when it sensed my presence at a distance, bent its neck and looked back. I saw fear in the bird's eye. I must not wait any more. I raised my single-barrelled gun and pointed it at the bird, which, I knew not why, shed the fear that was hovering in its eye, and concentrated on the water. I pulled the trigger and, like a pack of cards, the great white wings spread open and slowly fell to the ground. The bird did not move after that.

The sound of the gun was not loud, or perhaps it was, I could not tell. Because their nerves remain raw at the time of shooting, the eardrum of hunters, all hunters in general, do not register the sound of the gun. I snapped open the breech of the gun to clean the barrel and threw the used cartridge away. Hearing the gunshot Adina appeared near the mango tree with my sisters-in-law, who were waving their hands. I waved back.

And then I saw the black bird, perched on a thin shoot of bamboo that grew near the shallow water of a haff, the one that merged into the river Meghna, past the Chandhol bog. A big black cormorant it was, not even 20 yards away from where I had been. It twittered and fluttered its wet wings.

Its roosting, its movement, the dark black colour—everything emanated an aura of gracefulness, a sublime sense of pride. With a stare that spoke of circumspection, so natural in wild birds, it looked at me, and then removed its gaze to the haff. Forgetting Adina, who was standing far away, I started observing the bird. I liked the bird; its beauty; the spontaneity of its movement, perhaps, was like Adina's. I shifted my gaze from the corpse of the white heron floating in the water. I could not really fathom what resemblance the cormorant had with Adina. And at the same time, the more the bird dried its feathers, softly moving its neck from one side to the other, the more this idea grew on me that I had seen Adina move with such elegance and wonder. But wait, I told myself, Adina does not have a beak. At the same time, Adina was dark; soft black was the colour of my wife's skin. Only in their colour did I find a similarity between my wife and the bird. That gleam and freshness. Even though Adina was black, her skin had always glistened; that shine I now noticed in the dark shiny feathers of the bird, as sometimes the bright beauty of early morning dewdrops on the grass made me think of my wife.

When I got into Comilla Victoria College, a girl in a frock, affectionately chatting with my widowed mother in our front veranda, caught my attention. That girl was Adina, our neighbour Akil sahib's daughter; every Sunday she would come to our house to help Ma with household chores, or to pick lice from my mother's hair while licking a bar of pickles. Adina was at an age where girls have no inhibition about their body; how old was she then? At best ten or twelve. Or twelve or thirteen maybe, I was not sure. Though she looked awkwardly tall and thin, her arms and breasts were growing in bulk. So what, I thought when one day I caught a glimpse of her thigh through that short orange skirt: she was about to kneel to comb ma's hair, but my mother, seeing a crow hovering over some pickle that she had left to dry, ran to it in a hurry, and, I, sitting in the study, could clearly see the round mounds of her thighs, like two ornate pillars of some great building. I remembered being able to see them because Adina, while working, always pulled the short skirt up and knotted it before her navel like the way women wear saris.

She used to come to the study too; many a time, when I asked for a light to smoke, ma sent her with a match or a stick of burning sponge wood to my room. And after giving me the light, when she wiped beads of perspiration from her forehead with the frills of her skirt, I got a glimpse of her navel. It was like a chinarose in full bloom. Seeing it, seeing her navel exposed for the flicker of a moment, it occurred to me that it was necessary for her to have such a deep, thick navel to strike a balance with the awakening raw muscles of her stomach.

In its movement the black wet-winged cormorant resembled Adina so much that I could not take my eyes off it. Then it occurred to me that to shoot I had to get to the edge of the pond.

The bird was blissfully running its beak through its moist feathers;

careful though I had been while getting down to the end of the canal, my feet got stuck in the mud; I pulled myself along to halt near the edge of the water. Here I could load the gun. I felt relieved when rubbing my feet with a tuft of grass I wiped my feet off the sticky black mud, which was as thick as the outer skin of some animals. Before loading the gun I had a last look at the mango tree in my father-in-law's courtyard. Adina was still standing still under the tree in a pink sari, the one that had a black border; and Madina and Shakina, her two sisters, my sisters-in-law, hearing the gun, were running towards me. At first I thought I should let them come to me, but afraid that it would surprise the bird, I waved at them so that I did not have to get closer. My sisters-in-law stopped in the middle of the bog, they had understood that I was about to open fire.

I waited no further and went up to the canal, to the back of the cormorant, which was still combing its feather with its long slender beak. As the plumage of its tail had grown heavy the bird had blown its tail to dry; the swollen tail made it difficult for me to see the bird properly. Through the foresight of the gun I levelled my right eyeball with the bird while it embellished itself, and tried to steady my hands and hip to get a bull's eye, but was it possible to make the human body as numb as a slab or stone or a piece of metal? My single-barrelled gun, like my hands, was shivering. By then the bird had stopped combing itself, spreading its wing, it was contentedly staring into a school of small fish. It was about to fly off; this was the way widening both her hands Adina embraced me; only once; that, too, was six days ago. When our wedding night was about to turn into dawn, before my mother woke up to say her morning payers, I got up from the bed to open the door to go to the pond. Adina hugged my back and said, "Let us lie down for a while; I know you are annoyed with me, but believe me, it's the first day's blood, you would have been disgusted."

The way I had felt then—the shiver that ran through my body when I held her hands stretched open—that was what I was feeling now, seeing the wide wings of the cormorant through the foresight of the gun.

Then I put the gun down; no, not from any sense of affection, nor because of any stab of memory or moments of insight did I do so. I removed my aim from the bird because I was about to shoot it from the back, which no good hunter would do. I could not recall doing it myself before. Maybe those who rained fire saw no pleasure in not confronting their prey. Like the way men who spray semen into their women feel; what pleasure would have been there if one had not been able to see the bare face, naked arms, swelling breasts of the woman he was making love to? This, the spontaneity, the sight, the touch, leads to a sensation, a tightness in the body of the man till a part of his being, the one that solely devotes itself to pleasure, leaks out of him. He doesn't care whether or not this spray of pleasure will hit the reproductive tract of his woman. Those who spray gunpowder follow the same regulation—they stare at the visage; the breast; the wings; and the soft delicate curve of the neck. Besides, the cormorant had overwhelmed me; the bird was beautiful and that was why I wanted it. My fear was that if I shot at it from the back, the bullet would just brush past its wings, that I would miss the target. I stood still and saw the bird fold its wings and rub both sides with its beak.

When I turned round I saw that Madina and Shakina had started walking towards me. Probably after seeing me put down the gun they thought I had abandoned the target. Now if I waved at them to stop, it would startle the bird, and if I stood still like this, the two sisters' incautious presence would scare it away. Within a split second I decided to shoot; taking two light steps forward, I widened my legs: only eight feet away the bird was roosting on a young bamboo; even though I was still at its back, blurry though it was, I could see the bird. I raised the barrel of the gun again and opened fire. The sound of the bullet deflected by the bamboo hit my ear; right in front of my eyes the bird was flying away. Startled at first by the sound of the gun, the bird was now floating in the air, without any inhibition; and it dipped towards the canal, its wings fluttered for a while before they touched the waves of the canal. It flapped its wings, as though to get more strength from the action itself, and looked hither and thither. It spared me a casual glance, and then bending its neck like the curve we make with a needle while sewing, the bird entered into a wave of water. Left without words, I sat down on the bank of the canal, jealous of the place this wet black feathery bird had in nature, jealous of its beauty, elegance, grace, splendour; above all, its free spirit had left me in a state of wonder; I sat there with the warm steely touch of the barrel on my cheek.

On this side, on the green carpet of grass that sloped to the canal, Madina and Shakina were cleaning their feet of the mud. They ran towards the white heron when I showed the bird to them, floating on the knee-deep water of the bog. I smiled at these two girls' gaiety. They never immersed themselves in the wide overwhelming green of nature, neither had they ever drowned themselves in the ever-engulfing beauty of its vastness—the river, with a curve in its hip... the bog which was as wonderful and enchanting as a lake. On this green delta of flora and fauna, which on the map of the world looked like the womb of Asia, where, taking in watery air, girls blossomed into womanhood at the early age of nine, where women drew thick black lines around their deer-like eyes with kohl, where girls wore a round tip in the middle of their eyebrows, where girls walked free, their hair falling down their back like the frills of a tamarisk tree—in a place like this, why these girls' parents would spend their savings on building bricks or would go bankrupt while competing to make a city of concrete I did not quite fathom.

Was Adina still there? I shifted my gaze to the tree: yes, she was reclining at the foot of it. We had been married for seven days, so far no relationship—neither physical nor physiological—had developed between us two. On her first day at college she came to our house to touch ma's feet to seek her blessings. I was getting ready for work; after passing the BA exams I took up a situation in the local municipal office; my salary was 400 taka a month. Some said that it was easy for me to get the job because of my father, because, as he spent his life in the scavengers' department of that office, the mayor had taken a special interest in my case. After having breakfast I was shining my shoes when Ma brought her to my room.

"From today Adina is going to college, Anwar."

I looked up: Adina was wearing a light sky-blue sari with a deep white border. She bent down and touched my feet. She wore her hair in braids, and at the end of them there were two white roses.

I feigned surprise: "So Adina has grown up!"

Ma laughed and said, "You think girls grow up as soon as they wear a sari? Only a few days ago she was in a frock." "Yeah, how mature she looks now, look at her!" I said. Startled at what I said, my mother looked at Adina, who, seeing both of us examining her so closely, ran away, hiding her face in a handkerchief.

We started laughing, my mother and I. After Adina left, my mother said, "Such a good-natured girl, so lovely."

This was one bad habit that my mother had. Everything that pleased her mind ma would call good-natured; she did not mean the colour of Adina's skin, she meant her beauty. I did not dare to tell her that Adina was dark. And there was no point in telling her because I liked Adina too. I would observe her closely whenever she came to our house to see my mother, and every time she seemed to exude an aura of unquenched allure.

I said, "You would not like her if she was not good-natured."

Hearing this ma looked happy; turning round, she said, "What do you think of Adina, Anu, do you like her?"

Her question took me by surprise: what kind of liking is she talking about? I said, "Why, I like her, she is a good girl. She comes to see you; you love her dearly."

"Will you marry her, Anu?" she asked. I realised that ma's voice was soaked with pleading and happiness. I smiled and said, "I know it will be good for you ma, she will help you with the household chores."

Ma could not hide her emotion; she held my cold hand with her warm fingers in a fist. I said, "All right ma, talk with Akil sahib about it."

The cormorant was playing in the water: it kept floating up to the surface only to hide itself in the wave again. I looked into the wave that the bird was creating. Meantime, holding the bird's wings, Madina and Shakina brought the white heron to me. Their feet were again caked with mud, black like two pairs of gumboots. I did not realise that the bird was so big; when a flock of herons flew away from one bog to the other, birds as big as this one led them on. Madina and Shakina straightened its wings and laid it on its breast, both its green legs flattened like sheaves of young paddy in monsoon rain, blobs of red in its beak and neck.

Madina said, "You did not kill it in the right way. How will we have it if it is not halal?"

I laughed, "There is no problem: game and sea-water are always halal."

Bending her neck Shakina asked, "So there is no need to slaughter it?"

To assure the girls I said, "I fired in the name of Allah. Now it is up to you if you will have its flesh or not."

"We will, if only you have it," Madina said.

"There you talk like a Muslim," I smirked in reply.

The cormorant floated up again, this time near us. The girls went silent when I pointed my finger at the bird, and sat in the grass putting their hands on my back. They were hushing each other up; the touch of their betel-nut like unripe breasts and chin was on my back, the sweet smell of their hair in my nose. Embarrassed though I was, I realised their girl-like wonder at the pleasure of waiting. Resting their chins on my neck they were staring at the bird; it would have been better if they had left us, the bird and me, alone. I wanted to relish every bit of this moment—the movement of the bird, the flapping of its wings, its intent gaze. The bird did not let me do this—it covered itself with the wave again. Telling the girls to stay away from me, I fished into the pocket of my trousers and took out a cartridge. Both the girls, wide-eyed, saw me load the gun with equal enthusiasm; they looked round to see if the cormorant had floated up or not. The sun was striking down hard on us, the atmosphere of a dew-drenched morning was no longer there. I was feeling warm, though it was winter; drops of sweat were streaming down my forehead, which I wiped with a handkerchief, and cleaned the barrel, which, after this little attention was paid to it, was all brightened-up. The bird was visible again by the time I loaded the gun.

"It's there," Madina whispered in my ear. "I have seen it, now do not make any noise, the bird might fly away," I replied. But who would listen to this! My youngest sister-in-law, obtuse as she was, shrieked, "There it is, having a fish."

At the sound of Shakina's shouted words, the cormorant, which was probably eating a snail, went back to the water again. I was annoyed,

"Look, what you have done!" Full of regret, both the sisters started picking their nails. I could not but smile and said, "It's okay, now you two shall sit here silently. Do not talk. I will go forward now and shoot." They nodded and kneeled beside the white crane.

I went down towards the northern side of the bog, to the tilled land. A strange idea came to me, it had occurred to me that to kill the bird with one shot I just needed to point my gun and wait for the bird to resurface; I would open fire at the very sight of it. And that was what I did; resting one knee on the grass, and leaning the gun on the free knee like an expert hunter, I pointed the gun at the bank of the canal, where the bird was last seen and where it might reappear. I did not have to wait any further: like a black-carp, it floated back with a few slimy bubbles, and then I pulled the trigger. As I was dispassionate this time round, the sound of the gun hit my ears hard. I fell flat in the grass as the back of the gun struck me like a police stick in the collarbone. A plume of smoke sent out from the barrel could be trailed back from the bank.

At first, like a bullet-struck civet-cat, it moved in a circular motion over the edge of the water, then, its neck, levelled with the wave, thudded into the water; where the bird was fluttering now, it seemed, someone had poured a bucket of blood. I never knew that a huge swathe of the canal could become so thick and red with blood; I never thought that a cormorant would have such a huge quantity of blood to make it look that way. Oh the pain that the bird's red blood, its black feathers and the green water gave me! All of a sudden I realised that I had a headache; I held my eyes with the palms of my hands so as to spare my strained-filled eyes of this scene of suffering. If I had another hand I would have hidden my ears with it; as I had none, I surrendered myself and remained enchanted by the silent shabby squeaks of bleeding of this great black bird, so full of life, so rightly filled with a soul.

How long I had been hiding my eyes like this I did not know. Hearing Madina and Shakina's scamper I opened my eyes: Madina was hurrying her sister, "Go and fetch the bird, it might drown."

Shakina was worried that the bird might be lost in the water; I stood by her side and saw Madina hold the bird by a wing. The cormorant stirred, gentle though the movement was. Life was drained out of the bird; holding it gently to her breasts, Madina went up to the bank. She was wearing a pink frock, which was of the same pale pink as Adina's sari. She was drenched with water: the frock got stuck to her skin, and when she put the black bird down I noticed that, like some unripened exotic fruit, there were spots of blood on her black breast, as though two budding lotuses had been shivering at the chilly touch of an early winter dew-drop. Madina was shivering too; I said to her, "Take it off and wring it out. You might get a cold." She gave an embarrassed smile at first, and, turning round, took the frock off and squeezed it dry.

Spreading both its wings, the bird lay at our feet; the blood on its beak and breast had not thickened yet, lifeless though it was, because its eyes were opened, it seemed as though it would open its wings and fly away. Without batting my eyelids, I stared at the bird, my head and eyes ached. I could not keep my eyes open for long. Holding the gun in one hand, I slumped beside the cormorant; then, resting the gun in the grass, I hid my eyes with both my hands and in my mind's eye saw a circle, recreated that scene where the cormorant, so full of life and energy, was fluttering in agony over a wave of its own blood.

When I opened my eyes again I noticed that Shakina had laid the white heron beside the cormorant. Perhaps because of the contrast its colour had produced, the site of the tall white feathers gave my eyes a sense of relief. I told my youngest sister-in-law, "No more hunting today, let's go back."

On our way home, Shakina carried the white bird, and Madina the black one. I followed them. As happened to me often, the vein in my temple had swollen, I could not stand the sight of anything. I had seen my mother cry with such headaches, no tablet could heal it. When the pain became unbearable, I had seen her grind a kind of leaf, probably aloe vera, paste it to her temple and sleep. I had the urge to lie down now, there must have been an aloe tree in this village; I should tell Adina to pluck a handful of leaves for me. Thinking of Adina I stared at the tree. No, she was not waiting, let alone for the beak of the hornbill; no one would wait for so long even for Hiramon, the mythical parrot of the fairytale.

Our wedding took place without any hindrance; my father-in-law set only one pre-condition before me, he wanted the wedding to be held in the village, his relatives would be present there, and after the engagement and wedding party there would be a reception, after which we, along with the elders, would go back to Comilla. Only yesterday I came to my father-in-law's house for the reception, which we call "Firjatra" here.

Adina knew that I had bouts of severe headache, and seeing me return with swollen red eyes she asked, "Why are your eyes so red?"

"I have such a splitting headache, I must lie down." I replied.

"Let me wash your head..."

"Nah, I can't even stand still," I said and handing the gun over to her I went to the bedroom and fell flat on the bed with both my feet caked with mud. I felt as though I had entered a world of illusion. I could hear Madina and Shakina say something about the birds in the yard, where probably people had flocked together. I said people came to see the birds because I could hear them talk about the great size of the cormorant and make comments on how tasty its legs would be. Adina turned up in a short while and made me take two tablets for the headache, and I clutched at the pillow when she put my head on it. I could not tell her about the paste of aloe leaves for I knew she would laugh at such a remedy. While washing my feet with a strip of wet cloth she said, "There is a village-doctor's chamber nearby, should I send for him?"

"No," I said, "it will last a day anyway."

Before my words slipped out of my mouth my wife's father and mother entered the room. "Why do you not want to see a doctor?" he asked, "let the quack come and treat you. You went out in the morning with that gun in hand; I think you got a head cold. Being a townie you should not have walked in the wet grass barefoot. And you waded through mud and water..."

He put the back of his hand on my forehead. My mother-in-law suggested to Adina to put a strip of cloth with several folds soaked in water on my forehead to relieve the pain. I said, "Don't you worry, I often have this kind of ache. There is no need to call a doctor; I just need to get some sleep."

Before they left Adina's parents told her to make sure that I could sleep properly. Adina latched the door and while applying a strip of cloth on my forehead as her mother had suggested, she bent and took her mouth near my ear and said, "It's possible today. The thing has stopped."

I told her to sit in the bed and massage my head. Adina smiled and said, "You want it now?"

I held her in a tight embrace. There was no remedy to the pain, but when Adina hid my face with her breasts, in that immense darkness, which was as black as the cormorant's feathers, in the darkness of her breasts, I immersed my burning eyes to attain gratification. The feather-like darkness lifted slowly, as it happened after drops of milk were poured in a cupful of raw tea. Or the dawn-like radiance that one sometimes saw in a wide-opened pangash fish. I felt as though I could smell the birds that fly over the bog, as though I was enveloped by a soft comfortable gush of air.

Again I walked, armed with that single-barrelled gun, into the triangular bog, carefully stepping on the tender weeds. At the bend of the river I bent my legs and kneeled to shoot like a seasoned hunter. As soon as I sat, a cormorant, like a black balloon, floated in the water. I fired. The sound it made and the kick of the gun broke my vision of the beautiful landscape, in the blue background I saw a dark woman shaking violently in her own blood. It seemed this was a body—the luminous face, the arms, the breast, this pair of thighs—I had known for a long time. When I was about to call Adina, I realised, this body, so beautiful, so elegant, was slowly drowning in these giant waves. Pressing the warm barrel of the gun on my face I stood still, helpless, and my nostrils filled with the smell of gunpowder.

Translated from the Bengali by Ahmede Hussain

Interviews

An Interview with C.E. Chaffin

C.E. Chaffin with his dog, J. Alfred Prufrock, whom he describes as "my little English butler with a Japanese provenance."

B orn in Ventura, California, in 1954, C.E. Chaffin turned 54 in October 2008 and has white in his beard to prove it. He graduated from UCLA in 1976, Summa Cum Laudanum, Fine-Bit-of-Krappa, winning the top honors award in English, "The Edward Niles Hooker Award," though he was not in the honors program. He received other awards in medical school, in psychiatric residency, and later as a medical director. He taught Family Medicine at UCI and was named a Fellow of the American Academy of Family Physicians before the age of 40. Due to chronic spinal pain and manic-depression, he elected to retire on disability from medicine in his early 40s, which led to his discovery of the literary internet.

Chaffin published and edited the webzine *Melic Review* for eight years until its recent extended hiatus, a journal that has distinguished itself not only by its content but through the work of participating poets at its board in winning and/or placing in the monthly InterBoard Poetry Competition (IBPC) repeatedly. He has won one poetry contest (*Desert Moon Review*, 2002) and was nominated for a Pushcart Prize by *Rose and Thorn*. He quit counting publications several years ago but has been featured poet in journals over twenty times.

CTG: Could you say something about your influences? I know T.S. Eliot and Pablo Neruda are two of them. Do you wish to name any others?

CE: Jeffers, Frost, Strand, Roethke, Rilke. In mentioning them, I am naming poets I have consciously imitated. They are by no means all of my poetic influences, as opposed to poets I merely enjoy.

CTG: I was impressed that your book is dedicated to your late daughter, Rachel, whose death must have been a considerable loss and trauma to you and your wife Kathleen.

CE: If Rachel hadn't died, I wouldn't have dedicated the book to her. But the dedication to Kathleen would have stood. And isn't all poetry really a rebirth from grief? Spring is the season of poetry, even if Eliot mocked the tradition in "The Waste Land."

CTG: In regard to the demise of your web magazine, Melic Review, was it just the spammers that downed the site or were you having troubles (personal or whatever) that may have meant the end of the site in any case?

CE: It was three things. The barbarians overrunning the last civilized poetry board with no registration and thus no policing requirements; the failure to find a reliable webmaster; and my cyclical depression. But we were conscious about our end, and thus we called our last issue the "Death" issue, and published some fine work about death from a number of talented writers as our swan song. Incidentally, Chris, you are correct that the Melic archives do include some rare examples of my own poetry, although I want to point out that I did insist on never first-publishing staff.

CTG: I know you and your family lived in Mexico for some time. Do you want to say anything about your years in Mexico? I know your bio says you came back to California because your children were grown, but were there other factors? Why did you move there in the first place?

CE: Mexico was an experiment in trying to save your American home as a rental while living more cheaply in Mexico (we were house-poor). In this regard we failed. We came back because I really hated Mexico. I couldn't take the heat, even at 6,000 feet., and I was always getting sick with amoebiasis.

CTG: How did living in Mexico influence your poetry?

CE: I got a localized feeling for Eliot's "timeless moment" in the Amerindian culture of manana, although I think the imprecisions of living in Mexico would have driven Eliot crazy. Or crazier. I also read more Neruda and Paz and others in the original Spanish.

CTG: Now that you are retired from medicine, you both lecture on depression and lead one-on-one poetry tutorials. Would you care to comment on those activities?

CE: I'm a good guy to talk to if one is depressed. I have been there as a manic-depressive and also trained in psychiatry. Many poets have confided in me, which is to be expected, because, historically, about 20% of "name" poets are bipolar. It all comes with the territory: poet, doctor, madman.

I still tutor poets online, generally six weeks intensive for $300. I don't do it for the money but for the pleasure of encouraging new voices.

Fiction

Len's Basement

I.

He sits halfway up Mount Victoria, looking over the bay to the shore beyond. A brave few boats wobble uncertainly on the waves: fluffy little whitecaps spell danger, and an ill wind is whipping them up. The ferry stays safely moored. There won't be any crossings to Hutt today.

The wind doesn't stir only the water. The sky above is in motion, fat wads of cotton wool lolloping from left to right, over the land and out to sea. They move unevenly, jerkily, some bunches flying more rapidly than others then slowing to a gentle drift before picking up speed again. It's like watching music in the sky, he thinks. As if an entire orchestra were playing. Bass clouds, lumpish and sullen; alto clouds, light and flighty. Staccato full stops of cloud, punctuation, marking a rhythm. Motion, composed.

He feels it as well as hearing it, the music of the near-heavens, the melody of weather. It stirs him, as if he were playing it himself. One day, he would like to conduct the weather, to write songs for the sky and bay and clouds, create music to make the whole world dance. He crouches halfway to standing and starts to move with the clouds, to the time of the puffy beats. He feels the energy within him. It goes *zizz*.

No one can see him. He drops his trousers. He's still dancing, still feeling the seductive rhythm of the universe, somewhere much deeper than his mind, in all our minds, in the memory of ancient dances and camp-fires. He holds himself, he's so full he might burst. The music carries him and he carries the music, he leads it with his wand and the clouds go this way and that, building to a crescendo. He flies from himself: *scud-scud-scud*. In perfect time with the weather, the world.

II.

What am I doing here?

This town is smalltown. It's Saturday night, and I'm sitting outside the Matinee, drinking a bottle of—look at the label—Speight's. A local brew: golden, cold, tasteless. What may well be the town's entire smart set are sitting next to me, drinking suspiciously spritzerish looking cocktails and chatting about… it must be sport. Everyone here talks about sport, even the intellectuals. Is it rugby they play, or Australian rules? Union or League? I can't bring myself to care.

Nightlife on a Saturday for anyone under the age of twenty one on

Devon Street (both East and West) is a simple ritual. Get in your car. Get in someone else's car. Get in the boot of someone else's car if there are no seats left. Then drive around and around in an elongated loop that brings you past my table approximately every ten minutes. Stop your car occasionally to bang your hands flat on the hood of someone else's car. At about two in the morning, when I'm asleep in my lumpy hostel bed, have a fight. A loud, shouting, bloodless fight. Repeat weekly.

What am I doing here? Research would be the simple answer, yes, research. I'm researching documentary film material. A sculptor and filmmaker who lived in Christchurch, Wellington, London and New York. He never lived here, in this town, there's no personal connection, but he left his archive, all the bits and pieces, to the art gallery here, and I am researching them.

It's possible that this work could be done remotely, on the internet, through requests or loans. Oxford is a powerful institution: people would listen to a request from Oxford, they would say, yes, it's safe to lend things to Oxford, they would send me what I need.

It probably isn't strictly necessary to be here at all.

III.

'Individuality! Happiness! Now!'

The country lane is cut deep, sinking between the fields and hedgerows alongside. Centuries of feet and carts have pressed it down, making a rut, a channel for people, hops and corn. You can barely see over the top of the hedges; it's like being in a maze.

Only his little bald head is visible at first as he rides his boneshaker along the lane to the house, like a potato escaped from the fields; and then you catch glimpses of his figure, wiry and athletic, a pointy beard dipping from his chin, drawing ticks as he rolls over the bumps and potholes, conducting the landscape. Though nothing and nobody else seems urgent on this hot and lazy day, something faster than any of this is carrying him, like a little rocket along the road.

He's got it! He's got the idea, the idea that makes sense of it all. Free from the confines of his modern-wired brain, the brain that thinks of technique, of pounds shillings and pence, of the constraints of everyday living, his old lizard brain has broken through and made sense of it. DNA, the stuff that we are all made of, our timeless heritage, DNA is the Happiness Acid, the *zizz* in our very selves.

'Individuality! Happiness! Now!' he yells.

IV.

It's a short walk from the hostel to the gallery, up the hill. To my left, in the clear sky I can see Taranaki. A truncated cone, rivulets of snow still clinging to the wrinkles of its top, it's the perfect image of a volcano. It dominates the view from every part of this peninsula, it gives its name to the region. To my right is the Tasman Sea, and over the tops of the flat-roofed houses I can see the tip of his wand, a twenty-seven metre fibreglass reed that bends gently to the wind. A posthumous realisation of his dream, made possible with technology unknown in his lifetime. Though he was never its son, this town pays homage to him.

The archive is housed in the basement of the gallery, in a corner of the prep room, where huge postmodern artworks made of foam and plastic ketchup are being unpacked from their wooden safety crates ready for a new exhibition. Like all archives, it is in a middling sort of disarray. Packing cases hold components of sculptures he never built. One case, half-open, contains an orrery held together at the centre by his wife's wedding ring: less a gesture of romance than of immediate exigency. Glass cases hold slides and photographs. Sketches and philosophical ramblings are still roughly filed in his own shoeboxes.

They supervised me when I arrived, unsure what I was really here for, anxious that I might make the archive yield scandalous family secrets. A few conversations later they were as convinced as I am of the dullness of my task. During the war, before he departed for New York, he participated in the British war effort and made propaganda films, films about newspaper trains, and metal recycling. Quite a few notable artists and filmmakers put their shoulder to the wheel of the propaganda machine, made these quirky little war films, and this is what the book I am writing will be about.

I'm making my way through the shoeboxes, methodically, to look for any traces of influence or inspiration. I scan through some of the larger files, too. In one, I find sketches for a giant sculpture, fit in scale only for a Nevada desert valley. A rising walkway takes the viewer past spinning ribbons of sprung stainless steel that thunder and echo off the walls of the valley. At the head of the sculpture, you pass through a giant loop of the same steel to face the head of a snake. It spits a million volts of electricity.

V.

Even if you had the money, it's not so simple to build something as big as you want. Sometimes, the inherent properties of the material you're working with just won't scale. It's hard to understand why a two hundred metre loop of steel won't behave in the same way as a twenty metre loop of steel, why it won't *twang* rather than buckle and collapse upon itself, but it's something to do with the same resonant frequencies that make it so springy in the first place.

Looking out across these cluttered Manhattan rooftops, clustered with television aerials and rocket-like watertanks poised to launch into space, he imagines acres of impossible wands like grass or marsh reeds, swaying even with the low and sullen breeze that is all the city can summon today. Growing out of derelict lots on the lower east side like mechanical gardens, bud-topped stalks that with each dip and nod will talk to you of what mood the world is in today.

Even without the grass, he feels the city in his not-so-young bones, feels its dirty restlessness, its hunger made of hungers. He wonders if he should take a walk back down to the workshop and see how the scaled versions are coming along, but the thought of their tininess and meanness, of the expense even of the models, disheartens him. Maybe he should stay at his desk and write: perhaps another breakthrough will come, the old lizard brain might have something left to say.

Instead, he stays at the window and looks out across the city, his eyes skipping across the panorama, from skyscraper to skyscraper, like notes written on the clef of the island itself.

VI.

At the bottom of a shoebox I find a single piece of card. It looks as if it has been torn from a larger piece, and unlike all the other pieces of card which are full of restless little sprites and squiggles, this one bears only words. It says:

Individuality! Happiness! Now!

This will be the last Saturday night I spend drinking Speight's in the Matinee on Devon Street West, the last Saturday night I spend half-overhearing conversations about farming and taxes, the last Sunday morning on which I'm woken by the screams of illiterate hoodlums.

On Monday, instead of going to the gallery I drive my hired car inland, towards the volcano. Most of the way there, the farmland is so flat that it barely ripples with haystacks, rusting machinery and occasional clumps of volcanic rock thrown clear of the mountain's peak centuries ago. Eventually, I reach the conservation zone where the original kiwi bush has been maintained: on my walking map, this national park forms a perfect circle around the volcano. Suddenly tall dark-green podocarps reach for the sky; the road becomes overshadowed, a conduit snaking upwards through the forest. At the uppermost carpark I lock the vehicle. A small information hut and shop is open and I buy a bag of nuts and raisins before striking out on the trail. It's nearly noon.

Two hours later I breach the treeline and burst out into violent sunlight. The clouds are already below me, a solid white blanket reaching as far as I can see in any direction. The town, the gallery, the peninsula, everything is gone. It's just me and the mountain, me and the perfect volcano. I can see the first pockets of snow stuck in shadow behind boulders. My legs work like pistons, *shuff-shuff*, conquering the mountain. The thin air fills my lungs and with each breath it's as if I'm renewing myself. I've never felt so alive, so *present* in my life.

Above me, the cone reaches up and away. If I climb quickly, I can reach the top before dark.

She Looks at the Landscapes

The first one draws her so close, there is just the bumpy texture of the paint. Screaming yellows and civil blues and greys. Three steps back and it turns into a beach again, familiar in its yards and yards of gleaming sand, its milk and grey sky, its hemline horizon of sea. As indeed it should be, according to the postage stamp of a caption in the bottom corner, declaring *Pierre Blanche en Irlande.*

But there is no time for coincidences to bloom. The paintings should be flowers and she should be a bee, following them around the room, glutting on their nectar. A golden village on a yellow hill, edged by a cool border of lavender and the burnt green of trees. A blood-warm field with another hilltop cluster of houses, a hint of pink in the sky too, as though she is looking through a filter. A mustard field with a flaming trail of poppies down its centre. They look as though they are drowning, as though in another moment those scarlet heads will have disappeared beneath the grass sea.

How very Joan of her. As was this decision to sit on the floor, back against cool wall. Even the legs stretched out in front look like they belong to her. A new survival strategy?

She should have brought the green slip-on's in a bag. To hell with that, she should have insisted on wearing them, instead of these awful, awful lace up things. But she knows ammunition when she sees it. Her daughter.

'Shoe couture's hardly the point. If we pass a herd of sheep we'll be doing well.'

That one of Manhattan watches her now. Mean skyscrapers looming over smudged charcoal and burning yellow dots. Once she was one of those dots. She would have stayed there too, if she hadn't met Patrick there that summer. Married by the end of the year. Just like that, two fates snapped shut like a handbag clasp. Fast progress for a shy boy. Funny it's the park that comes to her now. Catching some young boy just before his bicycle skids sideways. The memory presents her alone, which seems odd. Still, in that moment she wasn't, not when all those people who happened to be passing smiled at the sight of the tubby legs wiggling in the air, her hands clasping the trophy torso, as the bicycle clatters to the ground. A couple of them even clapped. And then on, and none of those people ever sharing anything again.

More cityscapes, then some scenes of women in marketplaces from all around the world. She skims past these, forgetting all about being a bee. Of course, what she really ought to be doing is a little dance of joy down this sensible floor of oak or whatever it was. She had, after all, escaped

The Walk.

It was the heat, she decides, that caused her little outburst. At least, that was the last straw. Or the new straw to be more precise. After all, she was used to the intense conversations on things she knew nothing about—in this case the implications of the new French president on EU migration policy. She was even used to walking behind them or in front of them, as the path dictated. But that sun. Hammering down on them at four o'clock like it was midday. Even behind shades and a head scarf, a headache uncoiling itself. And the way they regularly slowed their pace for her sake, as though they were having a secret telepathic conversation about how annoying she was. In a way, that was exactly what they were doing.

The final ones take her out to sea. In the first of these, it looks as though part of the sea has turned into seagulls and is attempting to break away from itself. Into the rain too. It is not clear whether or not it will make it. Beside this, a fishing boat hangs half way up a wave, that curves around it like an enormous question mark.

And then she sees. The place she and the world carved out for her holds her no longer. Even if Joan had decided to stay living at home in her first college year, she was still eighteen years old now. She had her own life. As did he. As should she. She could do it all of a sudden, without any explanation. Like that time she dug up the roses in the front garden and replaced them with marigolds. His face. Like she was the wolf in Little Red Riding Hood, after swallowing his nice wife whole. That was when he taught his summer Thursday evening class, and she and Joan would feast on white bread and jam sandwiches and fizzy orange at the end of the garden, weather permitting. But leaving and not loving were not the same thing. She still loves him too, in a way, at least the side of him she fell in love with in the first place. The side that looked at her if she said something that didn't make sense or that wasn't fair to everyone concerned. Politely, humbly even. It always immediately humbled her. But that him, no matter how much it melts her, has all but disappeared.

Back at the doorway, a photograph of the artist greets her. He stands in a field in front of a mountain, the earth the colour of yellow autumn leaves, his canvas a mirror. Travelling the world for this collection. The fabulous life flutters in her mind like a moth in a shut hand. To his right, her reflection looks back at her, her face pale against the fire of his earth, his left shoulder nudging her arm. The trimmed bob surprises her. How long ago the salon of this morning seems. Novelty of hair being done without conversation.

Beethoven's Moonlight Sonata beeps from inside her handbag.

'How's the shopping trip?'

'Nearly finished now.'

'Right. Well, we're in that place we said we'd meet.'

'I'll be there soon.'

She snaps the phone shut, looks at the man in the photograph, as though expecting him to speak.

'You like?' asks the woman at the till, motioning with her hand towards the gallery.

'Oh yes. Thank you.'

'One moment, please.'

She turns back around. An outstretched arm, a white booklet dangling from a tanned, ring-laden hand.

'A gift for you. You see?' The woman flicks the pages and miniature versions of the paintings flash and blur into one another.

'Thank you,' she says, sliding book and postcards into her bag, careful so as not to bend the edges, removing a broken disposable camera as she does so to make room.

Across the road, the outdoor tables of a café are cluttered with people, talking or just gazing about them, enjoying aperitifs. The early evening sun is still strong. It shines through the leaves of a sycamore tree, dappling everything. The breeze caresses her skirt against her knees and the sides of her thighs. When she drops the broken camera into a bin, it does not make a sound. Something soft must have broken its fall. Just then, a car makes a U-turn right in front of her. A girl with long red hair, sitting in the passenger seat, laughs soundlessly amid the angry drone of horns.

And then she sees them. At the table at the very edge, where the road swings around the café and out of view. How could she have forgotten that was the place? Her first chance in a long time to observe her daughter unobserved. Untidy is the first word that comes. All those long almost black curls scraped back into a low ponytail that does nothing for her face, which is creased against the low, cloud-filtered sun she stares into, as though it is one of her mountains she is sizing up. They are certainly not discussing EU migration policy now. Both the gin and tonic and glass of beer on the table are untouched. He studies a menu with an expression of intense concentration. How silly of them to have a row. Children, the pair of them. Her family, who will be ok without her. Who will carry on, live their lives, like all the other people sitting outside the café.

She is too far away to make out the lines that glisten down each side of Joan's face, reflecting back the sunlight. She is too far away to see how, when Joan notices her mother and a smile startles her face awake, her eyes tether themselves to her. And she is much too far away to notice the small but growing bulge hidden for weeks now beneath those shapeless t-shirts. She steps forward, presses the round gleaming button and waits for the pedestrian light to blink on. Between them and her, the rush hour traffic crawls.

Marriage, Interrupted

They fought every day of their thirty-two year marriage, but not for a minute had my father considered leaving my mother. Remnants of love, habit, her ageless beauty (she must have made a deal with the devil), and maintaining the status quo each played their part to keep my father in apartment 2B on Yellowstone Boulevard in Queens. Everything changed when my mother left him and moved in with their friend Sheldon. Sheldon bore an unfortunate resemblance to the Pillsbury Doughboy, but made piles of money in Laundromats. My mother had been searching for a wealthy replacement for my father for years. To her, the fact that Sheldon was married to her friend Charlotte was of no consequence.

After a year of living alone, my father decided to leave New York. The apartment was downright depressing and his job in the garment center far too taxing for a man of sixty-two. Perhaps even more devastating was his belief that everyone, including complete strangers he passed on the street, knew all about how my mother had humiliated him. Fort Lauderdale seemed the perfect antidote.

In no time, he had a bevy of old beauties tempting him with homemade casseroles, club house movies, danish and coffee at the monthly dances, and invitations to early bird dinners for which he offered to split the tab. He enjoyed Florida so much, he bought the condo he'd been renting. Sidney had the life: pool and tennis days, a different woman each night. Decades late, my father was catching up with the sexual revolution.

He took a part-time job at the King of Poultry. Amidst the matzo balls and stuffed cabbage, against a never-ending soundtrack of Elvis's greatest hits, was a surplus of lonely female shoppers eager to get to know the store's silver-haired, handsome new clerk. The better looking women found a little something extra in their shopping bags—a slice of noodle pudding, a piece of derma, a couple of turkey meatballs—and he got a date for that evening. He sold a record-breaking number of barbecued chickens his first year there, keeping his boss happy and his libido rejuvenated. Abe Kleinman, owner of the Poultry King as well as president of the local Elvis fan club, was even considering making Sid a partner.

But trouble was afoot. My mother had not fared well in Manhattan since Sheldon's untimely death two weeks shy of their wedding day, and decided to test the Florida waters. She was determined to win my father back or, better yet, live in his condo while she searched for viable husband prospects. She flew down and called him on the phone from her room at the Holiday Inn.

"Sid, is that you?"

"Rose?"

"Yes, Sidney, it's me."

"You sound like you're right around the corner."

"I am."

"What do you mean? What are you doing here?" He looked anxiously over at Colleen Thompson, a petite blonde Presbyterian who sometimes got a yen for kosher food. She was placing the tuna casserole she prepared with Campbell's cream of mushroom soup and topped with Chinese noodles on Sid's small Formica dinette table.

"I'm thinking of moving down. I hear you love it."

"It's okay. Not for everyone though. Look, Rose, you caught me in the middle of something. Give me your number. I'll call you tomorrow."

My mother was disappointed, but still confident that he wasn't over her. She gave him her phone number.

"Speak to you tomorrow, Sidney," she said, hanging up the phone. Sitting on the faded, frayed bedspread, she surveyed the generic room. It was a world apart from the posh hotel suites she and Sheldon enjoyed before his sudden death, brought on by a life-long affinity for brisket with gravy, mashed potatoes and custard éclairs.

✱ ✱ ✱ ✱

Never dreaming my father would be anything but alone, my mother awoke early the next morning, allowing herself ample time to dress and make-up. Pleased with the results, she went downstairs and got into a taxi for the short ride over to Horizon Condo Village. Driving past man-made lakes and buildings distinguished from one another only by their number, my mother was not impressed. For now, however, she could not be choosy or she'd risk using up her dwindling savings.

She walked the two outdoor flights up to number three hundred and ten in building twenty-five and rang the bell. It took a few minutes, but then she heard footsteps approaching the door.

"Who's there?" Sid asked, evidently annoyed.

"It's me, Sid. Rose."

He opened the door a crack. "What are you doing here? I just woke up."

"That's when you used to like it the best. Remember, Sidney?"

"Jesus, Rose."

She pushed the door open and walked in.

"Not bad," she said, looking around. "Could use a woman's touch though."

Just then Colleen padded barefoot into the living room wearing Sidney's old plaid bathrobe over a black lace nightgown.

"Who the hell is this?" Rose asked him.

"Who the hell are you?" Colleen replied.

For once, my mother had nothing to say.

"You should've called first, Rosie," Sid said.

★ ★ ★ ★

The thought of my father with other women did not sit well with Rose. She lay awake at night in the cramped bedroom of her new, furnished rental at Lakeside Villas—which was neither a villa nor anywhere near a lake—and couldn't stop picturing him having sex first with one woman, then with another. One night she woke up panicked and drenched in sweat. In her nightmare every room in Sid's Horizon Village condo was filled with unmade beds.

While they were together, she had only disdain for my father; now she was obsessed with him. She began to stalk him. She lurked behind a clump of bushes when he was due home from work and watched as he escorted different women carrying Corningware casseroles and grocery bags up to his third floor lair. She put her ear against the wall of the laundry room, which was adjacent to his bedroom, but could only make out a word or two, especially when the machines were running. The moans, however, came through loud and clear, driving her into a frenzy. It took every bit of her self-control to refrain from breaking into his apartment and smashing the lovebirds with Sid's new seven-piece Teflon pot set. (She watched as he walked the empty box to his trash chute one night, and his attempts at homemaking without her drove a stake through her heart.)

She stopped hanging out in the laundry, but continued to call him and hang up at odd hours during the night, why, she couldn't really say. To hear his voice? Make him sick from interrupting his sleep? Stop possible lovemaking in progress? And she went to the King of Poultry, skulking around the parking lot, trying to discern which women he favored that day with an extra meatball.

She spent one entire night cutting my father out of every photograph in both of the albums she brought with her to Florida. She also figured out the code to his answering machine, (fifty-one, his lucky number at the race track), and called in to listen to his phone messages four, five, six times a day. She felt physically sick every time she heard a female voice confirm a date, "call to say hello" or tell him about the pot roast she just made. My mother was in trouble.

Never a believer in psychiatric care—or afraid, perhaps, of what she'd find out—she finally relented and went to see a shrink.

"It's really quite simple," Dr. Richman told her. "You're obsessing. You believe that Sidney is your property, always has been. No matter that you left him. Now that he appears to be managing without you, moving on as they say, you want to reassert your control. It happens all the time."

This did not make my mother feel any better. Valium, however, did. The doctor also advised that she move far enough away from my father to require a plane ride.

Back at her apartment, she studied a map of the East Coast. She didn't want to return to New York; it was too difficult to meet men there. Miami was appealing because of its abundance of rich, elderly men, but too close to my father. Deciding to rule out the entire state of Florida, she came upon Hilton Head, South Carolina. "Hilton Head," she said aloud. "Hmm, I like the way that sounds." My mother sang snatches of "One Day My Prince Will Come," as she pulled out her suitcases and began packing.

Meanwhile back at the condo, my father and Colleen were making plans to marry as soon as their snowbird friends came south for the winter. He had grown tired of dating and was ready to settle down again. For a nominal fee, he procured Horizon's main card room for their wedding reception. After a ceremony at a local justice of the peace, they'd gather with their guests for platters of miniature potato and kasha knishes and an assortment of Danish, all courtesy of The King of Poultry. Colleen suggested serving cold shrimp with cocktail dipping sauce, but my father blanched at the expense. They bought a dozen boxed wine coolers at Costco that they stored under their bed. After much deliberation, my father decided to throw in two bottles of vodka and a few quarts of orange juice. No one but he and Colleen drank the stuff; they would take whatever was left back to their apartment after the party. At the time I was twenty-four and living on my own in New York. My father called and invited me down for the celebration. Fearing that if my mother found out about the nuptials she'd attend the party and go berserk, he swore me to secrecy.

On a sunny Saturday afternoon soon after the start of the new year, I watched as my father married Colleen. The reception afterwards was a big hit with their neighbors and friends and, as previously decided with his partner, my father passed out twenty percent off coupons for purchases made at the King to all of his guests.

A month later my mother found out about my father's marriage from my cousin Joyce, who was always looking for trouble. But by then my mother was pursuing a wealthy octogenarian in the greener pastures of a Hilton Head condominium development.

Luck

A twenty-four-year-old Art History graduate student was walking home along Columbus Avenue, eating a slice of pizza after class, when six shots cracked out louder than any backfire from a car, causing him to drop his pizza in surprise. Two of the shots hit the back and head of Curtis Anderson, their intended target, a twenty-year-old black man in a red windbreaker who failed to come through on a negotiated drug deal with the shooter, who laid Curtis flat as he tried to run away across the crosswalk. One bullet hit fourteen-year-old Lasonja Burkett in the neck as she stood on the street corner with her friends for the last time. Two bullets went wild. The last bullet traveled an improbable distance down the block and through the lower right side of a thirty-two-year-old dark-haired woman who had just smiled at a gawky art student in passing, and her three-month-old baby's stroller rolled a foot or two away from her before he grabbed it and knelt by the fallen woman, stroller handle still in his hand. This was how I met Richard.

His brown eyes were huge with fright as he looked down at me and his thick brown hair fell down into them in a way that I would have thought was charming if he were helping me up after I slipped and fell on a patch of ice, instead of lying there after being shot. There was no pain at first, only the inability to draw breath, and the flat numb feeling after a fall where it seems as if your soul has been jolted from your skin for a split second. Then a sharp, stinging pain, like the world's biggest paper cut, only on the inside, and I gasped and cried out in a short burst when he asked me if I was all right.

"Where's my baby?" I asked him. He was trying to help me, taking off his scarf and holding it against my ribs to put pressure on the bleeding. He told me later, when I took him out to dinner to thank him for his help, that I just kept asking where my baby was, over and over. I remember only thinking through the haze of confusion and pain that I would lose her if I didn't pay careful attention. He told me she was right there, wheeled her around so I could see her through my panic, and I reached out and clung to her with one weakening hand, leaving a bloody hand-print on her yellow ducky romper that would need to be thrown away after. He told me I would be all right, even though he privately doubted, and gave me his hand to squeeze while he held down the scarf with the other, and corralled the stroller with his foot.

Maybe he felt noble, comforting a pretty woman as she died, or possibly he hoped I'd recover and shower him with gratitude and *my hero* kisses. But this was no romance: I was married, happily so although not in the stereotypical or gaudy way of a movie or romance novel. I met Ei-

147

tan when he was seventeen and visiting from Israel for the first time with his parents. They were Orthodox but not obtrusive: the father was a tall man in a suit and a fedora while the mother was a lovely dark woman with an embroidered scarf. I would later find out that the mother's family was Palestinian and their relationship had been something of a scandal. Eitan was their youngest, the second of only two boys out of six, and the family was quite wealthy from an import-export business. The father had combined a business trip to peddle olives to upscale New York vendors with a college tour for his youngest and brightest child.

Eitan had the striking and exotic good looks of a child born to two attractive but dissimilar parents: Palestinian and German coloring combined and clashed to leave him with brownish-red hair, creamy off-white skin, and cheekbones with the razor sharpness of a letter opener. He was tall and had grown too fast, his weight unable to keep up with his sudden upshot in height, and he would have looked like a scarecrow if he hadn't had the sense to wear Eurotrash, closely-fitting but not too tight clothing.

He was bored, hanging out by the subway while his father attended a meeting, and he stopped me and asked how he could get to the Empire State Building. He spoke perfect English with a heavy accent I couldn't place. I had just picked up my deli lunch in a sack and was heading back to my downtown office building when he asked, and I offered to ride with him until his stop. He told me about his college tour during the ride, hands flapping with his exuberant telling, and I offered to show him around the city over the weekend and told him I was twenty-two when I was really twenty-five.

I was angry with my fiancé for little annoyances, like always putting the empty milk carton back in the refrigerator and using the last of the roll of toilet paper without getting another from the closet. It was my first time living with someone and I had yet to realize that these were minor, expected frictions, and didn't constitute firing offenses. I had started searching the want ads for a new apartment, and instead, this was my petty revenge. Eitan was a virgin in that Orthodox way, where all the girls he met weren't even supposed to *touch* a man until they married him, and I would have slept with him at some point during his week in New York, but we could never get his parents to go away from the hotel room and my place was out of the question. Instead we gave the guards an eyeful on the security camera in the elevator of the Sheraton, going up and down the fifty floors overlooking Times Square while we made out and Eitan got his hands either up or down the different shirt I wore on each particular day. I could have rented my own room in the same hotel, but it never occurred to me.

He wrote to me, after he got back to Israel, told me when he got accepted to Williams and Wesleyan and Stanford and Columbia but didn't quite make the cut at Harvard, Yale, or Princeton. By the time he arrived at Columbia the following fall, he was eighteen and had successfully lost his virginity during a summer trip to Ibiza (and apparently expanded on this knowledge with several subsequent girls), while I had married Peter, the reformed live-in boyfriend who made a renewed effort to buy peanut butter *before* he ate the last of the jar. This marriage would last three years before I discovered Peter having an affair with his secretary and the marriage dissolved in the face of the affair, as well as my inability to get pregnant after two years of trying. Peter later dumped the secretary for a masseuse, and may have worked his way down the food chain to a stripper by now, I wouldn't know because I stopped speaking to him. You could do that after a divorce that involved no children.

I took Eitan out while he was in college, to lunch or a movie, telling Peter that his parents were friends of my family, and that he was a lonely kid by himself in a strange city. His Israeli accent faded over the years and he stopped growing vertically, expanding to a normal width that lessened his resemblance to his Auschwitz ancestors. He was a senior and twenty-one when he spent the night with me for the first time; we got married when he was twenty-three. Eitan was twenty-five by the time I got shot, barely older than Richard the art student, but a successful man with a wife and a new baby, one that arrived in the face of my lazy refusal to take birth control since it was so obviously unnecessary. We were delighted and surprised by her, less surprised and more delighted as time went on.

Paramedics poured out of the two ambulances that arrived first on the scene, maybe ten minutes after a handful of observers called 911 on their cell phones. Richard's scarf was soaked with blood and I drifted in and out of consciousness when two of them came up on us, with their heavy red paramedic toolkits. One was an older man, with neatly clipped white hair and beard, who looked like he would have made a good and kindly priest. The other was young, with blond eyebrows and obviously dyed-black hair and tattoos snaking up his neck out of his uniform. They took over, shining light into my eyes and getting an IV going, even as they were still checking for the extent of my injuries.

The young one played good cop, talked to me in the soothing, cooing tones I used on my own infant. He asked me to tell him how I was doing and I asked for my baby again, he'd pushed her just out of my sight to make room for the paramedics to work. "She's right here," Richard said, pushing the stroller back a little closer so I could see, so I would stop struggling against the paramedics to reach for her, wriggling quick and slippery as a fish. The young paramedic said she was a beautiful baby and asked me her name. I told him—Salomé, Eitan's and my private joke with the world—and he asked me what my name was and I told him that as well, Brielle.

"Brielle Harris?" he asked, pausing with his gauze.

I told him I was and he was impressed. I should have guessed: I wrote a moderately well-known series of mystery novels, in which a dominatrix named Yolanda (Yoli to her friends) solves crimes in her spare time between erotic romps, with the assistance of her on-again, off-again boyfriend, a Santeria priest named Jean-Pierre, and her lively Siamese cat, Lux. I also wrote a less popular series about a group of spicy fairies in Chicago and their ongoing eternal war with the Chicagoland vampires. There was a time I considered myself a *real* writer, wrote endless Carveresque stories about the insignificant hurts of everyday life, before giving it up as useless and actually making some money. Under normal circumstances I might have expected Tattoo to recognize my name, as there seemed a direct correlation between black hair dye and my popularity as an author. As it were, he treated me with new gentleness and looked at me with wider eyes after I told him my name.

When they loaded me into the ambulance, my helper said he was my friend Richard and he'd better come along and bring the baby. It was the first time I'd heard his name, served as an introduction of sorts, and he handed Salomé up in her stroller before getting in himself. When she cried, the older paramedic scowled, but Richard lifted her up and hummed to her. Later he told me that this was the first time he'd ever held a baby that wasn't related to him, and he worried that if she cried I would struggle to hold her. He sat towards the front of the ambulance, holding her near my face so I could see her, and I kept crying and apologizing to the paramedics for crying but I just couldn't help it, and they told me I was doing great.

At some point he called Eitan. I don't know how he figured out to do it, but he looked at the dialed calls of my cell phone, tucked in the front pocket of the diaper bag, and saw that most of my calls were to a number for "1Eitan," a designation I gave him so he'd be first alphabetically in the address book, so he called him and said he was my friend Richard and Brielle had been in "an accident" and that we were on our way to Columbia Presbyterian emergency room. I couldn't hear Eitan's response, but I heard Richard lie to him as he said, "It's not so bad," and he hung up and said Eitan was on his way.

They wouldn't let him into the operating room—they asked if he was my husband and when he said no, they said no. They wouldn't let Salomé in either, and I argued, lifting myself an inch off the stretcher with a momentous effort as if it were a hundred inches. Richard said he'd stay with her, and by then I trusted him with his earnest brown eyes, although he could have been waiting to steal her to sell on the baby black

market, but he said he only had her by himself for three nervous min-
utes at most before Eitan burst through the emergency room doors and
Richard knew this was her father by the reddish hair and sharp-edged
nose they shared. Being the man he was, Eitan thanked him, didn't say
who are you anyway or *she doesn't have a friend Richard*, instead he shook
Richard's hand and gave him a business card.

When Richard called the cell phone number from the business card
later that night, I was up in my room, recovering from surgery where
they patched me up and removed part of my badly damaged small intes-
tine. The entrance wound was a small, neat circle but the exit was a big,
torn gash that required 21 stitches. My gravest danger was from septic
shock, as the small intestine is a nasty little swamp that spews bacteria
and toxins when ruptured. After the recovery room, where I was still
groggy from anesthetic as Eitan kissed my hands again and again and
told me how he couldn't lose me, they moved me upstairs and gave me
lovely, lovely painkillers, something akin to morphine, and I drifted in a
dreamy haze as Eitan told Richard I was going to make it and thanked
him again and this time thought to ask for his contact information.

It was a week before I came home from the hospital and almost six
weeks before I called to invite Richard to dinner. In the weeks since he'd
last seen me, I'd lost quite a bit of weight, something I'd been meaning
to do anyway since the baby. Three of my books appeared briefly on the
low end of the bestseller list for the first time, after my picture was on
the front of newspapers the day after the shooting, me looking very goth
and exotic with pale skin and dark hair in a book jacket photo, Curtis
Anderson and Lasonja Burkett looking very young in their high school
picture-day photos. I'd had my stitches removed and seen the small,
sunburst-shaped scar on my front and Eitan held a mirror so I could see
the scar on my back, which was shaped like a kiss.

When I saw Richard in the restaurant, I didn't recognize him, like his
face never existed, and all I remembered was the way he held onto my
hand, and the way he kept little Salomé Harris-Hoffmann with me so that
she could be left home with a sitter by her *two* parents. He wore scuffed
shoes and looked confused at the preponderance of forks. We bought
him the most expensive meal he'd ever eaten and he told us about his
studies, looking embarrassed whenever we told him how grateful we
were.

This is what you did for me, Richard, in the seconds when you decided
to stay with me, instead of going about your business, or going over to
gawk at the other victims, like most of the rest of the crowd who watched
that fourteen-year-old girl gasp her life away on the sidewalk. Probably
I wouldn't have bled to death even without your putting pressure on
the wound. I don't believe a paramedic crew would have abandoned

a three-month-old baby in its stroller on the street. But you got me through, when you didn't have to, and when I thanked you for it, gave you a last, ginger hug after dinner, you said anybody would have done the same thing, and I said I doubted it.

The Principal of Rivington Street

He was an educated man. Today, no doubt, he would have been a university professor of some renown, but in those days a grade school teacher was more than respectable. Louis Bloom, through hard work and dedication, became the principal of P.S. 20 on Rivington Street. There, after the Great War, he made a career, and apparently was content. Why he chose to upend his life in such a way was incomprehensible to everyone except Bloom himself.

Now it so happens that Public School 20 had some illustrious graduates. Mostly, they were Jews who emigrated from Eastern Europe at the turn of the century to escape a pogrom, here and there, or fathers avoiding conscription into the army, or the general promise of a better life in America. Edward G. Robinson and Paul Muni, the film and stage actors; the future Senator, Jacob Javits; George and Ira Gershwin; and the journalist Harry Golden all attended P.S. 20 around the same time. Quite a graduating class.

Edward G. Robinson and others, well-known and not so well-known, were Rumanian Jews. They were congregants of the First Romanian-American Synagogue, Shaarey Shamoyim (Hebrew for Gates of Heaven), also located on Rivington Street at number 89. At its zenith, it had a seating capacity of over 1,600 people. And it was, if I may use the word, a Mecca for all the great cantors of the day, and nurtured the careers of operatic tenors Jan Peerce (nee Perelmuth) and Richard Tucker.

This dizzying proximity to such an overabundance of talent was most likely the cause of what they later called Louis Bloom's deep descent. Certainly a man takes stock in his middle years, particularly a bachelor, but a career as a singer in show business? No, just not done. Intellectually, Louis Bloom understood he was an educator, but in his heart he was a *hassan*. Unfortunately for Bloom, the really bad part was he couldn't sing, not a note.

Bloom had many fine qualities: A first-rate mind, a dedicated man who gave all his attention to the task at hand—perhaps too much attention. These days he might even be called an obsessive personality. He wrote in a notebook every detail of life in his school: The number of seats in each class, the pieces of chalk sitting on the sills of blackboards, a count of the halls where chipped paint had become a problem; and most importantly, the names of the teachers' wives and children, their ages, hair color, habits if any—and there was a special place in the notebook reserved for everything he could think of or notice about his students. In this way he hoped to be liked, to be paid attention to.

In the sixth year of his tenure as principal of P.S. 20, his diligence appeared to wane. He often was not available in the afternoon, and this was noticed by his staff. It was gradual at first. People thought perhaps he had become ill, but it became clear his focus was elsewhere—what had been a helpful obsession, that is his work at the school, had turned into another, darker, secret, magical obsession.

Once a week, later twice, and eventually even three times, he walked to Houston Street where he took the subway to the 42nd Street stop at Broadway, paid his admission, and was mesmerized by the singers, dancers, comedians and novelty acts at the Morosco theater. For weeks he would attend the matinee, delighting in the same acts over and over again. He was so engrossed that P.S. 20, for that period of time, didn't exist for him. At a certain point, it became an absolute necessity in Bloom's mind to meet and talk with the show people who plied their magic on stage.

On a sunlit November day, in the middle of the week, he stayed for four shows. It was a drab winter night when he finally left, but he did not go home. Instead he went to the alleyway behind the Morosco. He waited in the cold until a trickle of vaudevillians emerged. He tipped his worn, black felt hat to each in turn. The few women who emerged shuttled past quickly without acknowledging him, though a few of the men nodded to him.

Life turns on small points. And when Bert Savoy, the female impersona-tor—who Bloom immediately recognized—emerged from the shadows of the stage door, the scrawny principal straightened up as he had when called to attention in the 119th Infantry Brigade of the American Expeditionary Force. As Savoy, with a man's swagger and the swish of a woman, came close, Louis Bloom spoke. It was more of a surprise to Bloom than Savoy.

"Good Evening, Mr. Savoy," Bloom said, with surprising equanimity.

Slipping on his lambskin gloves, and without paying much attention to Bloom, Bert Savoy responded. "Good evening, good evening."

He was well past the principal when Bloom almost shouted, "Wait, there is something important that I must say to you."

"... Yes?" Savoy sighed audibly, stopped and turned around.

"First, I want to say how much I admire you and your great talent. I have seen you many times and am always enthralled... There is some-thing I need to say, and I'm not sure where or how this entered my mind. Or who placed it there. I am not a wholly religious man, but I can only think it is He who placed it there."

"Come, come, man, what do you have to say?"

"I fear for your life."

Savoy blanched. "And why is that? Is it perhaps you that means me harm?"

"No, no, please believe that. It comes to me as a daydream, but more real. It is so hard to explain. I am not a criminal so you should have no questions about me. As I said, I admire your talent—and I, even at my age, wish to be on stage. But I am compelled to tell you this, even at the risk that you'd think me a lunatic."

Savoy was outwardly calm, but he did not move on. He himself had had forebodings, which he was not about to share with Bloom. He was known on the Orpheim circuit, vaudeville's most prominent, as someone who had an uncanny knack for prediction. Although he now worked as a single, his ex-partner, Joe Brennan, claimed Savoy was psychic. "What is your name?"

"Bloom. Louis Bloom, principal of school P.S. 20 on Rivington Street."

"And what do you see about me, Mr. Bloom, eh?"

"I would not want to talk here," Bloom said. "May I buy you a glass of tea?"

Savoy laughed a genuine hearty laugh. "Tea?! I'm a female impersonator on stage, Bloom, but that's where it ends. If it's gin you are offering me, that's another story. I'll hear you out and hope we both don't have the same premonition."

They walked to a nearby saloon in silence—each wanting to speak, yet shards of anxiety kept them silent. Once inside the speakeasy, The Club Napoleon, a spectacular Beaux Arts mansion, Bloom was awestruck by the interior. Club Napoleon was quite a famous gin mill known to everyone, except, apparently, to Bloom. The principal's eyes seemed to scan the place in two directions, one eye looking this way and the other taking in a wholly different portion of the plush, oak-paneled great room, with its portraits of the famous and the dead. Bloom, since he was a child, had had a thyroid condition that created the illusion, in times of stress, that he was looking in more than one direction at a time. His eyes also tended to bulge disconcertingly.

Even taking into account this disturbing continence, Bloom was completely out of place at the Napoleon—both in his slightly disheveled appearance as well as his bearing. Yet Bloom was beside himself with excitement. This speakeasy, that Bloom had known nothing of, and would most likely cost him all the money in his pocket, was filled with entertainers and Broadway hounds. He thought he recognized half the crowd. "Is that George Raft?!" Bloom asked, half an octave above his normal speaking voice.

"No, it's Sophie Tucker in a tux. Now sit down and order that drink you offered. And get something for yourself… and for Lord sake don't order tea. My reputation is at stake here, Bloom."

There were two gins delivered to the table, then two more, and after that another two. Louis Bloom was woozy drunk, which was a decided advantage for Bert Savoy, as long as Bloom didn't pass out.

"All right, Mr. Bloom," Bert Savoy said in a quiet determined tone, "what do you see for me?"

"Water."

"Water? Are you too drunk to carry on a conversation? Would you like water?"

"No, I see water. I see you and water and darkness. Something very ominous and you are there in my daydream... and there is water and death."

Savoy sat silent, staring at Bloom for quite some time. "How long have you had this daydream as you call it?" he finally asked.

"Long enough. Ever since I envisioned myself as singing at the Gates of Heaven Synagogue, and, of course, at the Morosco theater like yourself."

"This is all the world needs, another singing Jew. You would think Jolson and Cantor would be enough." Savoy shrugged, gesturing that he meant no offense. "Well, that aside, Bloom, I want you to tell me—how long has it been?"

"You mean my premonition, how long? Several months now."

"And it always involves me? Always?"

"Yes. You and the water. I'm afraid so"

"Gypsies have portents of the future. Is it the same with Jews?... Bloom, I want you to sing for me."

"What? Now? Here?"

"Yes, now. Maybe you *are* a lunatic. Sing. If you have some talent then my own thoughts about the future may be true after all. But I believe you have none and I am known for my intuition, Mr. Bloom."

"Please, Mr. Savoy."

"Bloom, Sing," he commanded in his best stage voice.

"...Well, I do know *Tea for Two*."

Savoy lowered his eyes. "Tea again. All right, go ahead and sing it then."

By the time Bloom got to *'Just me for you and you for me alone'* Savoy abruptly cut him off. His eyes lit up and he grabbed Bloom by the shoulders. He bellowed with great relief, "Bloom, I am right, you are a lunatic!"

"What, you didn't like it? I am a little nervous with all the noise and George Raft is right there. Was it so bad?"

"Well, Bloom, let's just say you're not ready for the Morosco quite yet... and maybe not ready for premonitions, either."

"I wish with all my heart that was true. The premonition, I mean."

"Bloom, let me tell you something. In spite of myself, I like you. I just hope your premonitions are like your singing, tremendously off-key. But I must confess I've had my own uneasy feeling about the future, my future. Honestly, I couldn't see one for myself. But now I'm relieved and all because of that lousy singing voice of yours." He raised his glass and toasted Bloom with the last of the gin.

They were quite an unlikely pair, the flamboyant entertainer and the intense school teacher. Bloom continued to come to the theater, and Savoy was not particularly upset when Bloom was waiting for him at the stage door. They ate together on more than one occasion—Bloom enthralled by the great female impersonator and Savoy smugly satisfied with pointing out the principal's shortcomings.

Bloom was in Heaven, so close to show business. Burt Savoy even talked about the possibility of Bloom playing straight man to his former partner. "I want you to meet Jay Brennan," he said, "then we'll see."

"When?" Bloom inquired.

"On a Monday, I suppose. The theaters are dark Mondays. That is if you can make it? And I'm not promising anything. You'll just meet him and see how it goes."

Although he had received two inquiries from the education board regarding his work, he brushed these aside. "In the late afternoons on Mondays, I can get away. Where will we meet? Will it be soon?"

"Slow down, Louis. Maybe in a few weeks. At Luna Park. Brennan's a juggler on the promenade, temporarily of course, but he's a gifted comic. He needs a stooge for his new act, Bloom, and you won't have to do much.

"This means a great deal to me, Burt."

"Don't get soft on me now. If things go okey-doke, I'll even treat you to one of those kosher hot dogs from Nathan's Famous. And it won't cost a nickel, either. Cantor, me and Durante lent Handwerker the money to open that place. I bet you didn't know *that*."

"You're a good man to help Jews like that."

"Sure, what do you think? We all worked at Feltman's restaurant together before the war... And, besides, I'm helping *you* aren't I?"

★ ★ ★ ★

At first, Bloom was on top of the world, his heart filled with a joy he hadn't experienced in years. Yet the principal found it difficult to sleep, and his daydream now invaded his non-waking hours. Nightmares with that water, and Savoy ending up badly. Bloom, a man of profound focus, found himself nervous and adrift.

On a morning a few days after the American New Year, Bloom realized what he must do. He would go to the Gates of Heaven synagogue and seek the advice of the Rabbi. He thought to himself, 'the Rabbi is a wise man and will be able to help rid me of this fear, or at least explain what it all means.'

An imposing Romanesque Revival style building, the Gates of Heaven synagogue on Rivington Street conjured up thoughts of a medieval castle. Bloom stared up at the great stone archway, hesitated, and reluctantly entered. Inside, the synagogue was magnificent and elaborate. The sanctuary was extremely wide with a huge gallery extending deeply into the great hall. Magnificent stained glass windows and an intricate chandelier reminded a man to whisper in such a place. So Bloom, who viewed himself as inconsequential, quietly tiptoed into the study where Rabbi Yaakov Singer had agreed to see him.

There, behind a mahogany desk, the Rabbi looked up at Bloom and smiled. The gentle manner belied his Rasputin-like appearance. When he stood up, he was nearly a foot taller than the principal, and Yaakov Singer's piercing brown eyes had the facility to call up biblical wrath when needed.

"Louis, I'm glad you've come. We so seldom see you these days."

"I know, I know, Rabbi. I've been preoccupied."

"Preoccupied how? Are you ill, Louis?"

"No. That is I'm not sure. I want to change my life, what I do for *arbeit*, for my work." Bloom looked away. "And, I... that is... I also have a foreboding, a vivid daydream, that stays with me. This, I am hopeful, is your domain, Rabbi." With that, Bloom proceeded to tell Yaakov Singer, in great detail, all about Burt Savoy, show business, and his great unease.

The Rabbi listened intently. When Bloom had finished he looked toward the Rabbi who remained silent. Finally he asked, "Do you have for me advice, Rabbi?"

"About these hallucinations, I have no advice—but a caution." His sharp brown eyes were now wide and his speech urgent. "This is fire that you deal with here, Louis, of which nothing good can come."

It's *water*, not fire, Bloom thought. "Rabbi, please."

"Remember what I've said, Louis." The Rabbi stroked his beard for a moment, then shook his head and softened, the gentle smile returned. "All right, all right. This I will tell you: These show people are not men like you and I. There is something in their minds that is quite different. They live for fame and attention. They have no understanding of the true life. They are incapable of contemplating His plan."

"All show people?"

"Yes"

"Even the Jewish ones?"

"Especially, the Jewish ones." He was expressionless for a moment, then laughed softly, placed his hand on Bloom's shoulder and walked him toward the study door. "In the Talmud, if a man finds his father's lost property and his teacher's lost property, that of his teacher takes precedence. Although his father brought him into this world, his teacher—

who taught him wisdom—brings him into the life of the World to Come. *Fairstast?*"

"I think I understand, Rabbi." He did not, really. It's water not fire, Bloom thought to himself again.

"Good. Then return to teaching, Louis. Resume your duties full-time. You will be at peace, believe me."

★ ★ ★ ★

Coney Island was especially warm for an early March day. It had taken Bloom just over half an hour on the recently built elevated BMT subway line to reach Surf Avenue, and the entrance to Luna Park. The entrance was directly on Surf Avenue and Bloom craned his neck in search of Burt Savoy. People of all sorts bustled past him, and beyond the entrance the crowd mingled with one another on the promenade. Bloom waited for twenty minutes and still no Savoy. The principal thought he must have missed him in the sea of faces around him. But Bloom was determined to wait. Burt Savoy was too good a man not to keep his word.

"Hello, Dearie," a voice called out from behind.

Bloom turned around to see a woman in a flowered print dress, smiling at him. At first he didn't recognize her, yet the face was familiar. In an instant, stunned, Bloom, made a great whistling sound as he swallowed a gulp of air.

"Yes, it's me. What do you think?"

Bloom couldn't speak. "It's okay, Dearie, I'm out for a promenade," Burt Savoy said, pressing his hand on Louis Bloom's arm. The principal jumped back, ashen.

"Oh, come, come, Bloom, don't be absurd. It's a game we play, Brennan and me. Who can make the other laugh. He'll show up and see me, and he'll act as though nothing is out of the ordinary, as though nothing is different. He won't show a hint of emotion. He won't give me the satisfaction, but eventually he'll crack up... or I will. So don't get all tussled, Bloom."

Bloom was all tussled, and didn't quite believe Savoy's story, a man he thought he could trust. All right, Savoy was a very tactile individual, but his touching and grabbing made Bloom extremely skittish.

"Well, where is he then?" the principal demanded.

"Who knows, I guess I'm not psychic after all. Louis, relax, consider me on stage"

"That's fine for you, but I'm all new to this. And did it occur to you that's the ocean there, the water?"

"I'm not going in for a dunk, Louis."

"He never goes for a dunk. A bit too much lipstick, don't you think?...
Well, hello boys," a neatly dressed man in a straw hat said.

"Ah, Jay, here you are. See Bloom, you have to admit this fellow has
great timing. And you don't know the half of it, Dearie"

"...Hello, Mr. Brennan," Bloom said sheepishly.

Brennan gave Louis Bloom the once over, then looked over at Savoy.
He let out a rollicking laugh. "You win Burt, you always win." He was
still grinning. He came close to Bloom, looked straight at him. "You want
this green pickle to be my setup man?" Brennan placed an arm around
both men and shook his head.

The clouds had rolled in so quickly no one really noticed. The sky
became black. Bloom, for his part, was both embarrassed and angry, as
angry as a mild-mannered principal was entitled to become. He grabbed
Brennan's hand from his shoulder and pushed it aside.

The last thing Bloom saw before the lightning strike was the look of
surprise on Jay Brennan's face. Lightning was quite unusual in March.
Later, they said the principal lay on the ground for only a few minutes,
but it seemed like hours to Bloom. He had felt the hair on his body
stand upright, and a gust of something knock him to the ground. Not
wind, mind you, but a force of energy that made him nauseous. His eyes
bulged, and they said he scanned the emergency room in two discrete
directions when he was treated at Coney Island hospital.

The principal was released late in the afternoon, pronounced in rea-
sonably good health and told to rest for a few days. When he inquired
about Burt Savoy and Jay Brennan, he was told matter-of-factly by the
attending that they had been electrocuted instantly.

Bloom took to his bed for more than a few days. What had he done?
Rabbi Singer was right. About entertainers. About fire. He had strayed
from the path assigned to him. He had involved himself in depravity and
had relinquished his responsibilities. Louis Bloom considered he had
brought upon himself a catastrophe, and worse, a Holy wrath.

With this revelation, Bloom became a wholly religious man, an obser-
vant Jew. He spent time in synagogue and listened intently when Rabbi
Singer spoke. The principal also contacted the education board. He told
them he had been ill, was recently discharged from Coney Island hos-
pital, and would resume his full-time duties at P.S. 20 in the following
weeks.

It was close to the end of the term when Bloom returned. He con-
fidently walked the halls of P.S. 20 as he had done for so many years
before. He smiled at students and staff. He was resigned. And when he
gazed upon those students who would soon graduate, it was not a look
of pride, but of disdain. Who among them would sing at the gates of
Heaven?

The Best Of The Society Pages

T he Cabots speak only to the Lodges and the Lodges only to the Lord, at
least that's what mother told me. I've had more than a passing interest
in the social calendar ever since. And this season, for me at least, has been
the most significant and momentous in memory. Below are a few highlights:

30 PRESENTED IN RYE

Thirty Women from Westchester County were presented last night at
the Eggs-Over-Easy Debutante Ball in Rye, New York. In a traditional
ceremony, each woman received roses and a small island off the Greek
coast.

Proceeds from the annual event will go to The Fund for The Recon-
struction of The Eisenhower Administration.

MOREHEAD SNEAD CAPTURES CUP

In one of the most exciting finishes in memory, Moorehead Snead III,
skipper of *Impervious*, crossed the finish line some thirty seconds ahead
of the sloop *Hegemony* to win field yachting's prized Skeffington cup. In
field yachting, a sleek, single-masted craft is pulled along a polo field
by day laborers known as 'sloop caddies.' The first yacht to traverse the
field and cross the goal is declared the winner.

Moorehead Snead III, an overrun specialist with the Lockheed Corpo-
ration, and the crew of *Impervious* clearly ran the tactically superior race
and were never headed by the opposing yacht, *Hegemony*. *Hegemony*
had its problems from the start as it strayed off course and interrupted
the second chukker of a polo match being played on an adjacent field.
Seven ponies died in the incident.

SARAH OGDEN ROOT TO BE BRIDE

Announcement has been made of the impending marriage of Sarah
Ogden Root to Osgood Stegman Jr., a lobbyist for the Poppy Seed As-
sociation, currently seconded to the Ministry of Agriculture in Kabul,
Afghanistan.

Miss Root, who is currently engaged in experimental salmon farming
in her condominium in Aspen, Colorado, graduated from Miss Porter's
School and holds a Master's degree from Columbia University. She is the
great-granddaughter of Zachariah Root, an Assistant Secretary of the
Interior in the Coolidge administration and inventor of the aluminum

shovel.

NORTH KOREAN OLYMPIANS TRAIN IN GREENWICH

In a whirlwind display of swimming pool diplomacy, the exclusive Greenwich Country Club hosted sixteen members of the North Korean Olympic diving team. Less than forty-eight hours after their Ilyshin II-14 touched down at Kennedy International, the divers were in the water.

A few member of the club, unaware of the invitation, complained about 'Asians flailing about in the pool.' Sin Sun Ho, North Korea's Permanent Representative to the United Nations, assured the group that his government will reciprocate later in the year. U.S. divers will be invited to use the facilities at the Glorious Fissile Enrichment Pool located outside of Yongbyun.

MUFFY ELIZABETH LODGE TO WED HEBREW

Mr. and Mrs. Steven Shriver Lodge of New York and Kennebunkport, Maine have made known the engagement of their former daughter, Muffy Elizabeth, to Henry F. Mazel, son of Abe and Ida Mazel of Bay Ridge, Brooklyn.

The future bride, an officer with the private banking house of Brahmin Brothers, Saks and Forrester, graduated Smith College. She was presented at the 2003 Debutante Cotillion and Christmas Ball, and recently was asked to resign her seat on the board of the Daughters of the American Revolution.

Mr. Mazel, the future bridegroom, is a merchant associated with the Pitkin Avenue Herring Works, as was his father before him.

September Rain

A faint remnant of the long, hot summer lingered in the early October evening as the man and woman emerged from the fine dining restaurant, comfortably arm in arm. The male was a portly figure with grey hair that held only faint traces of the black mane of his former youth, with a round clean-shaven face and a short nose, upon which rested a stylish pair of silver-rimmed glasses. He carried himself in a gait stiff with pride; though occasionally there was a decided wobble in his step. The female companion was of medium build and moderate height, with long brown hair and an ovular facial structure that was a vague extraction of the man's. Her laughter was boisterous. She had a firm grip on his arm as the two exhibited an obvious familiarity.

"Hey, how about you let me have the keys," the woman requested with a good-natured smile as the two made their way unsteadily across the macadam parking lot.

"It's okay." The male assured with a dismissive wave of his thick hand.

"You've had too much to drink."

"I know my limits. I'm fine."

"Dad, let me have the keys, please."

"What, and have you drive my car? May I remind you that this baby isn't even a year old yet. Besides, you're no better off than I am."

"I only drank two glasses of wine," the woman protested. "You've had four scotches and a cognac."

"You were keeping track?" he asked, brow furrowed in incredulity. "Did you also happen to count the calories in my dessert?"

"I think you've had a just a bit too much to drive."

"Wendy, I'm almost sixty, not sixteen. Don't you think I know myself by now?"

"You seem a little tired."

"We're both a little tired after what we've been through this week."

"Look, I've just lost my mother, I'm not about to let anything happen to you, or me, for that matter. Make both our lives easier and hand over the keys."

∗ ∗ ∗ ∗

When they heard the diagnosis they were not wholly surprised. After occasional bouts of illness over the past half decade, if anything was going to cut down the energetic and vivacious heavy-smoking dynamo that was Sonia Schiff it was going to be cancer. Still, there was a tremendous disbelief when the lung cancer was deemed terminal and the death clock had been started. It didn't seem possible that there was going to be a time when her infectious laughter did not fill the house, but the cancer had developed so profusely that no amount of treatment: conventional, homeopathic or otherwise, was going to prevent or even postpone the inevitable. They had to come to terms with the fact that one was going to lose her mother, the other the love of his life, and from that very moment it changed the way the father and daughter related to one another.

"I don't want you to stand in your father's way when I'm gone. Let him be his own man." Sonia commanded as her daughter kept a bedside vigil.

"Do you think I could?"

"All I'm asking is for you to not be overly judgmental if he moves on with his life. Your father's still a young man."

"Christ Mom, you're still in his bed, yet you're talking about the next woman!"

"It's just a possibility I want you to be ready for."

"He loves you. The way you're talking it's like he's going to be chatting up women at the funeral."

"I know he loves me, but I'm not going to be here. I know your father and he's not going to want to stay in this house all by himself."

Another woman in the family home, cooking at the same stove as her mother, sitting by the large fireplace in the den, sharing his bed, was one of the many incomprehensible possibilities that Wendy Schiff was struggling to absorb.

✶ ✶ ✶ ✶

"This is ridiculous," the father protested. "Will you just shut up and get in the car."

"I will not." The defiant woman pulled away.

"Come on, let's not spoil a lovely evening."

"I agree. Let's not ruin things by getting killed."

"Jesus Christ, Wendy. Can't we just go home?"

"As soon as you hand me the keys. It's only four miles."

"The fact we're arguing about this proves you're flagged."

"I am not!" the father protested, pushing up his glasses.

"You are not driving, and that's final. Now, don't make me lay on the hood."

"Shit, and I thought your mother was stubborn."

"I'm not stubborn, I'm tenacious, and I got it from you."

"You're right. You are stubborn, otherwise you would have come to work for me years ago."

"Oh, here we go again!" Wendy sighed, slapping her thighs.

"What's wrong with a father wanting his child to join the family business?"

"Construction has never interested me, you know that."

"There's no other field where you can get the satisfaction of having built something that will outlast your life. Thousands of children were educated in the schools my company built. Just think of those churches; the weddings, funerals, and baptisms that took place in something I helped create, all the lives touched, people I never even met."

"I wanted to find my own way."

"Well, you have found your way, always have, ever since you were that wiry and precocious kid who ran puppet shows in the back yard and roared like a carnival barker. You've proved to yourself, and to me, that you are a success. I'm very proud of you, so come with me now and run things when I retire."

"I'm an accountant, I don't know anything about building. You want me to cast aside the client base I've been building for almost a decade and jump into a completely new field?"

"Well, yeah. It would be a challenge, but I know you love challenges. We have a great team in place and I'd be there to ease you into things. I wouldn't just drop you off and say, 'here, run this ten million dollar-a-year company.' You'd have to learn how things are done, step-by-step. First we'd start off by seeing how you do with making the coffee and go from there." he winked.

"Are you listening to yourself? You must be drunk. I mean, what are we doing, playing out the scene from The Empire Strikes Back?"

"What are you talking about?"

"Join me and we can rule the galaxy as father and daughter. All this because you didn't have the son you wanted."

"That's not true and not fair." he said with a correcting wave of finger.

* * * *

As much as Greg Schiff loved his darling little girl, it was a painful blow when Sonia announced that she could not bear him any more children, not another precious girl, or the son he longed for to carry on the legacy of Schiff General Contracting. The company, which had been started in May of 1934 by his father, William Schiff, as a one-man masonry contractor, specializing in laying up block foundation walls, had grown into a respected firm that employed thirty-five field and office staff, and it had been his dream to see his children follow him into the business that had been so good to the Schiff family.

William Schiff had been an enterprising man with a friendly face and big ideas, attributes that were not always trusted in the years following the depression. He had a belief in himself and the great country into to which he had been born, and his optimism was infectious. He knew that being trustworthy and getting people to believe in him was going to be the key to his success, so he took his tools around to many of the local builders and offered to do his best for them. He was given a chance to prove himself, which he did through long hard hours of toil and craftsmanship.

Word of William Schiff's skill, honesty and proficiency began to get out, and after two years he was able to hire an assistant, a laborer who would do the unloading and mixing. Within five years he had four employees and was working from an office trailer. By the tenth year he had built a home, which would serve as the business office for the next twenty years. When Greg Schiff joined his father in 1973, they were just getting into development work and purchasing land for residential subdivisions. At present, the company was one of the largest homebuilders in the county and owned seventy acres of land zoned for commercial use, where the long-term plan was to develop the site for office and retail use. He had hoped to pass on the good fortune to the next generation of Schiffs, but with no children in the business there was an acute sense of pointlessness now.

$$\ast \ast \ast \ast$$

"Your mother was the stubborn one," Greg Schiff recalled, leaning against a black SUV. "I could never get her to cave in. Once she set her mind to something—that was it, she was intractable. The first thing I'm going to do tomorrow is throw open all the windows and air the house out."

"Mom loved her cigarettes," Wendy reflected. "Remember how she used to sit by the fire, smoking, sipping wine and reading her Danielle Steele books?"

"She would sit in that chair of hers for hours on end. I hated leaving, especially at night, but she insisted I go to those planning commission meetings. 'I need a little peace and quiet,' she used to say."

"Your civic duty called. Besides, it gave us girls a chance to talk. I'm going to miss those conversations."

He took his daughter's hand. "I know it might not seem like it, but I worry about you."

"I'm fine, Dad."

"I want you to have somebody special in your life. I don't like you being alone."

"I'm not alone—I have you."

"You know what I mean."

"I used to worry about finding a man, but now wonder what I would do if I had someone and lost them as you did Mom. How are you going to cope, Dad?"

"By taking things one day at a time. I learned long ago that life itself is no different than running a business. You treat others as you would want to be treated and appreciate what you have achieved. Success is measured by how you confront the day-to-day challenges. Sometimes you win and sometimes you lose, but if you meet and beat the problem of the day the victories become cumulative, and when you look back you suddenly realize you have a track record."

"I like when you get all philosophical."

"Is that what you call it? I thought you were going to call me pompous."

"Not at all. I love you, you do know that right?"

"Of course I do."

"I didn't think I could again, not after the affair."

"Do we have to bring THAT up NOW?" Greg Schiff groaned.

"I'm just saying you mean a lot to me, even after everything that's happened. I was a confused young girl and you really hurt me. When you ran around with that woman behind our backs you violated a trust and made me question everything I thought I believed in, everything that was rock solid. Sometimes I wonder if that's why I'm so unlucky in love."

"That was a long time ago, a mistake I regret to this very day. I know I disappointed you, not to mention your mother, but surely you don't blame me for your romantic situation?"

"You don't know what my romantic situation is. For all you know, I could have lots of men in my life," Wendy blustered but soon deflated. "No, I don't blame you for my romantic situation, or lack thereof, and I don't mean to come across like a resentful bitch. I guess I'm just being the tough little daddy's girl."

"I raised you the best way I knew how, and that probably meant treating you like a son sometimes, rather than a daughter, but I was only trying to pass on what I knew as a man. I've had very little experience being a woman." he smiled weakly.

"Were you disappointed that I wasn't a son?"

"Not at all. I have always loved you. If you want to know if I'm disappointed not to have had a son, then that's a different question. Your mother and I tried having other children after you were born, but after she'd suffered two miscarriages, the doctors said your mother would never be able to carry another child to full term. That's when I was disappointed. I was disappointed in her. There was a time when I thought she couldn't be the woman I needed or deserved, and that problem was with us throughout our entire marriage, but we dealt with it day to day. I admit, I wanted a son, someone to craft in my own image, to take hunting and share all those unique manly things, but that's just ego, I guess."

"I've tried to make you proud."

"And you have. Your mother and I are very pleased with the amazing person you have become."

✶ ✶ ✶ ✶

"I want Uncle Dan to be one of my pallbearers." Sonia Schiff instructed with a commanding wave of one of her beloved cigarettes.

"After the way he acted at your Aunt Florence's funeral?" Wendy protested, recalling the drunken escapades and the police lights.

"Dan was just sending the old bird away in the best way he knew how, and he's sure to do the same for me. And then there are the hymns; we have to find something more uplifting than Amazing Grace. I don't want everyone standing around crying the whole time; I want them to have a little fun. Maybe you can pick out something nice by the Beatles. Oh, I can't believe I'm sitting here talking about my own funeral as lightly as if we were discussing recipes."

"Dad and I just want everything to be the way you would want."

"It's weird to be planning your own party, one which you can't possibly attend." the frail woman choked amid a burst of tears.

"It's okay, Mom." The child said, looking away. She could barely stand to look at what the cancer had done to her mother's body. The woman was like a ghost already; flesh pale and hanging alarmingly from her thin frame.

"Sometimes the reality of this thing overwhelms me and it's hard to take," she gasped, regaining her composure. "You know, I'm not a religious person. I believe in right and wrong, but not necessarily some all-powerful being. There's too much evil suffering in the world for there to be a god, but I've found myself praying every night 'please, just give me on more day,' and the next day comes and I say the words all over again, 'just one more.' I don't know who or what is listening, but I say it all the same. I pray for you too."

"Me?"

"I had hoped to see you married before I slipped away."

"I'm sorry that hasn't worked out, but George Clooney has been busy."

"There's no need to be sorry. I just want you to be happy. What about that nice boy, Paul Becker? He was really sweet on you there for a while."

"Mother, I haven't heard from him since he went to Philadelphia to finish pharmacy school. That was ages ago. He's probably married with kids by now. I'm fine. There's no need for you to worry."

"I'm a mom, it's my job to worry."

"Don't. I'm not abnormal or anything. I just haven't found the right man—yet. Who knows, one day the miraculous might happen, and I'm sure if the day comes you'll be looking down from above, commenting on my dress. Enough about my party already. What about yours? Can you think of anything else you would want to have?"

"Whatever else happens, don't let Aunt Pat get up to tell that story about me and her and those two brothers from New York!"

★ ★ ★ ★

"Your mother loved this place," Schiff said, staring at the candlelight flickering through the windows of the old stone building. "She said they served the best filet mignon. We were here for Valentine's Day. I didn't imagine it was going to be her last."

"I keep wondering what Christmas is going to be like without her. She really loved the holidays and made them so special."

"I was thinking the same thing. All I know is, I'm not decorating the house like she did. That's way too much work. Maybe we should go away for the holidays, make a total break from tradition."

"That could be great." Wendy agreed. "Where would we go, London? Paris? Rome?"

"I was thinking more like Tampa, but an overseas adventure might be fun. Are you sure you wouldn't be ashamed to be seen with an old drunk like me?"

"That's ridiculous. You're the one that's going to have to put up with me and my book fetish."

"After living with your mother for thirty-three years I'm sure I can manage you for a week."

"I'm going to miss her so much."

"I know."

"I never realized how close we were until she was gone," Wendy said, eyes welling with tears. "How I needed to share things with her."

"Well, we can't sit here all night, kid."

"I don't know, it's been kinda nice," the daughter sniffled.

"Yeah, it has. Hey, why don't we call a cab?"

"In that case, we may as well go back inside and have another drink." Wendy suggested. "To Mom."

"No doubt about it, you're my daughter all right!"

Greg Schiff took his child by the arm, and together they headed back into the restaurant, to remember the past and forget the future.

The Tonight Show

G uys would get off the B-52s and go straight to the chow hall, causing lines that stretched out the building onto the perfect British paved streets of Diego Garcia. It took almost an hour of waiting in line for me to get a Cornish hen, a square of green beans, a rectangle of lemon pie, a kindergarten size dehydrated milk, and some ice water without ice. The guy across from me was an E-4, the faded crow on his sleeve needing stitching, and he kept looking at his plate like he didn't have a friend in the southern hemisphere, so I asked who he was stationed with. He said nobody and he looked just like Jay Leno. I said you have to be stationed with something, and thought, Jesus Christ, if Jay Leno was in the U.S. Navy he would be right here in front of me, that big chin pointing straight down, straight at pie, straight to hell. He said he was a photojournalist, just back from Kuwait. He said he took a great photo of an oil rig burning and said fire has every color in it and he could play with the shot and make those rainbows come out and he might have something big, real Bravo Zulu material. He put his head back down to soup up his lemon pie and spoon green beans. There was too much clanking silence in that loud room full of hushed crew cut Air Force officer fucks and scroungey dungareed Seabees and needle-nosed MPs and dumb-ass CTs.

But I couldn't let it go. So I said it, told him who he was identical twins with.

Jay Leno looked up from his beans and his watery lemonade and then his plate levitated, and he crashed it down, a one second food fight, specks on everyone near our table. Only one glass broke. Filipino janitors and E-2s could clean that up. He walked off, the boring disappearance of another human, most of the tables taking about as much notice as if he'd yawned, loudly farted, excused himself.

I finished everything on my plate. I had another thirteen hour night watch less than forty minutes away. I was going to do it off two hours sleep.

Shooting

I like courts with no nets, just a bent rim and gravel, a court business-men couldn't even find on the map, courts with graffiti tags on walls and swing sets where girls never seem to come. I like to be alone when I shoot around, for it to just be me and God and my imagination, pretending it's game seven in the finals and I'm some unknown sixth man coming in to replace Rasheed or Tayshaun, and the dead tennis court in the distance is filled with fans. I like to feel raindrops when I shoot threes, prehistoric clouds on the horizon, when weather has some threat and I know nobody else will show, just me and a 75 cent thrift store Rawlings. I like how my hands get callused from dribbling for hours on end. You don't need any money for basketball. You don't need equipment or friends or good weather. I like to shoot around during the first snow when your fingers hurt if you dunk and it's hard to get a foothold because of the ice and the town lights come on to save you from the dark, the rim barely made out, shooting at where you think the rim is but you're not sure, hoping moonlight will grace the ground. I like to play hard by myself after finding out Jon got shot in the lower back in a driveby in west side Flint on La Grange where he shouldn't have been. I don't care if he was visiting his cousin. Idiot. I like the pain in my side. And being the only white guy for miles. And how pigeons never come down from the sky to rest here. I like being rescued from the unhappiness of life for a few hours every day, an addiction. If I was a millionaire, I'd have a court in my backyard, but I'd be amazed if I ever managed to somehow make more than $12,000 in a year, which I haven't been able to do and I'm 35. I'd get a gym membership and see what it's like to play everyday on polished wooden floors with the echoes on the walls and scoreboards, but I have a feeling the novelty would wear off and I'd return here with the sidewalk over to the left and the barbed wire wall to the right and in the middle this place where any time I want I'm invisible.

...Five, Six, Seven, Eight

A gentleman of about 60 years of age sat dozing in a wheel chair. The blue flannel robe he wore was the same blue as his eyes, which he opened periodically only to close them again. The warmth from the sun streaming through the solarium and the glare from the snow were conducive to dozing. Each time he dozed he dreamt of a place or a time that upon waking would seem familiar, but he couldn't exactly remember it as being part of his life. Each dream was like watching a movie.

A ranch house with a well-tended lawn in a neighborhood of other ranch houses and well-tended lawns in one dream, in another, a cheerful woman, in jeans and an apron in the kitchen baking cookies while four fair haired boys ran through the house. He thought he was one of the boys, but couldn't remember which one or what was his name.

Every day he had these dreams. Sometimes he was older and there was a dark-eyed girl with long dark curls in his dreams, the girl with the laughing face. "Let's race," she would challenge and run off, sometimes winning, but always laughing, even when she lost. Sometimes they were kissing, sometimes they were at a football game or a school dance, or at a funeral. Someone's mother or father. Funerals and weddings. Laughing Girl in a bridal gown. Was it his wedding? He didn't know.

"Mr. Marshal?" A woman in a starched blue smock was tapping him awake. "Time for lunch. Mrs. Marshal will he here later. Perhaps she can take you outside if the sun stays out. You'd like that, wouldn't you, Mr. Marshall."

Was he Mr. Marshall? He stared at Blue Smock who looked familiar, but from where? He tried to rise from his chair.

"I know you want to walk, Mr. Marshall, but the dining room's too far. You got to go in the wheel chair."

The routine was also familiar, like he and Blue Smock had done it many times before, like a long run play. He sighed and did as he was told, wishing he could cancel his performance.

"Did I tell you I saw you on stage once? Frankly, I couldn't afford the tickets, but they were a gift. You shouldn't have let those theater people charge so much. Who can afford it unless you're a Rockefeller? Do you understand me, Mr. Marshall? Do you even hear me? The doctors say we should all talk to you. Part of your therapy to get you to talk again. So, like I said, I saw you on stage with... "

Oh, he heard her. He heard everyone. Just didn't always understand what they were talking about. He looked up and blinked at the spotlight. He blinked again. No spotlight. No stage. Just the sun off the snow.

Blue Smock had put him in an old wheelchair today, the kind with wooden arm rests and wooden wheels and a large, comfortable cushion. Leaning his head back he rolled with the wheels. Rolling, rolling. Like a train. Rolling across country. On the road with Laughing Girl. One town, then another, playing the same show. What was her name? What is *his* name? Blue Smock called him Mr. Marshall, but that didn't seem quite right.

The girl with black curls called him Sammy, pulling him back on stage. "Come on, Sammy. Take another bow."

Applause. Applause. Flowers tossed.

"This one's for me," Sammy said, catching a bouquet of daisies. "Just a humble flower for me."

She laughed—like pealing bells—and thrust all her bouquets into his arms.

Applause. Applause.

"Here we are." Blue Smock's voice broke into his dream as she wheeled him into the dining room. It was a cheerful room with flowered curtains on windows that gave a view of the snow covered grounds.

"Hello, Sam," a wrinkled old woman with frizzy red hair called from one of the tables. Blue Smock stopped the wheel chair next to her. Was he Sam? Laughing Girl called him Sammy. Nothing matched up to his dreams.

Also sitting at the same table was a fat, bald man who, looking up from his food, mumbled "Hi ya, Sam. Can you believe this food? Just tuna salad with lemon. I like mayo."

"Lemon's healthier. "Frizzy Red moved the dish closer to Sam, as if he were a child who needed encouragement to eat.

She wasn't Laughing Girl, not if Laughing Girl were a real person and not someone who came only when he slept. He looked at the other people in the dining room. No one looked like the girl in his dreams. Maybe that's all she was, a dream girl, a product of his imagination.

"Mr. Marshall, your wife is in the solarium waiting for you. Blue Smock was back, but Sam shook his head. He wanted to walk. He didn't want to be treated like an invalid, like a child who needed watchers. He was... He was... He didn't know what he was.

"I'll tell you what, Mr. Marshall. You ride in the chair until we reach the solarium. Then you can walk. O.K.?" Sam nodded.

At the entrance to the solarium, Blue Smock stopped the chair and motioned another Blue Smock to give her a hand. With one Blue smock on each side of Sam he was helped to his feet and began a slow shuffling walk. He had done this before, not this slow shuffle with the two Blue Smocks, but before that. It was... it was with Laughing Girl. And a slim man who wore a penguin suit, as he did. Laughing Girl was in red spangles, glittering across the stage with him and Slim, shuffling, not like now, but with a rhythm. ... *five, six, seven, eight.*

"Easy, Mr. Marshall," Blue Smock said. "Take it slow. Yeah. That's right."

"Was he counting?" Blue Smock Two asked. "I think he was trying to count."

A woman with silvery hair waved and began walking toward him. Sam didn't know her. Her hair shimmered in the sun, the waves brushing her face reminding him of someone, someone with black hair. She had a smooth walk, her long legs seemingly not touching the ground, a dancer's walk. Now, why did he think *dancer?* She smiled, but it was a sad smile, not like Laughing Girl's smile. It was forced and didn't succeed.

"Hello, Sammy darling."

Sammy again, but this woman had silver hair not dark. Yet... He sensed that he knew her, not just from her coming before to the solarium, but from before that, from way back, from a real life and not a dream life.

...five, six, seven, eight... Once more...*five, six, seven, eight...*

"He said it again," Blue Smock Two said. "He's counting. I heard him say *seven, eight.*"

Sam dragged one foot forward, then another, straightened his back and came face to face with Silver Hair. She looked troubled and reached out to take his arm. He pushed her hand away and shuffled another step, paused and took another. ...*five, six, seven, eight.*

"I heard it too," Silver Hair said. "Just now. He is counting. Oh, Sammy. You do remember. "She stood close by Sam, but didn't touch him, as he made his slow way toward a couple of wicker chairs. "Remember, Sammy, the marquee's and posters? *Sammy & Lydia Marsh.* Our last name shortened so as to fit, but always on top with *Chuck Taylor* underneath. Both of you in white tie and tails and I in a sparkly dress. Remember the rehearsals and how many times we practiced our routines?"

When they reached the two wicker chairs Sam allowed her to help him sit and put a pillow behind his back. "Sam...y. Lyd...a Mar..." He studied her face, watching a smile appear.

She took his hands in hers. "Yes, yes. Sammy and Lydia Marsh. You remember." She squeezed his hands and laughed, a bell pealing laugh that rang clear and sweet. "You remember and you're talking and walking."

Improper Burial at the First Iron Works of America

W ith one glass eye and with one wooden leg, but with a shovel in his hands, 72-year old Napoleon deMars was an earth surgeon. But he felt cold and clammy when his long-handled shovel painstakingly pried up the buried object. It was disinterment! White of bone came at him, from the grave. It was a human skull, opened at a wedge in the frontal lobe, and Napoleon knew it most likely had been murder. The skull, and apparently some of its bones holding on to the last known form, lay at the end of his half day's work, a trench at the First Iron Works of America, in Saugus, a mere dozen miles from Boston's Freedom Trail. The site was being excavated for and from history. It was September of 1952. Excavation had been under way since 1948, on a small scale, but steadily. Not a single piece of diesel-driven power equipment had been allowed in there as yet. It was a pick and shovel site, a whiskbroom site, toothpick and cotton swab country.

Now it was a graveyard.

Napoleon, for all his years, for all his toted calamities, felt nauseous.

Three people of varying importance were at the Iron Works site when the grisly discovery was made: Napoleon deMars, the seventy-two year old, one-eyed, one-legged earth surgeon; Dr. Roland Wells Dobbins, site archeologist who had found the ruins of Thoreau's cabin at Walden Pond a few years earlier, now in charge of unearthing the site of the very first iron works which had brought to America all the experience Europe was able to muster back in the 1600's; and Silas Tully, police officer of the town, on the force only a matter of six years after his service in the Marine Corps in the once-noisy Pacific.

On that high-blue September day, clouds laying over someplace else, the faintest breath of salt coming off the river, at eleven o'clock in the morning, Napoleon deMars put down his shovel. It was a half-hour to lunchtime and he never stopped work, he never cursed his place in life, he never gave cause to any boss. Here, at the Iron Works, at $2.35 an hour and the best wage he had ever gotten, where he often thought that he could shovel until he was eighty, he put his work aside.

He looked out over the First Iron Works in America, up off the banks of the Saugus River on the North Shore above Boston. The site was a conglomeration of excavations, mounds, slag piles, marked stone walls which had been retrieved from history, a half dozen trenches cutting across a small piece of Saugus crooked as lightning, ragged as crossword puzzles, and the scattered piles of artifacts yet to be catalogued and put away.

Napoleon walked up the site with the marked limp he had carried with him for more than half a century. The broad band of a suspender hooked over one shoulder and slipped into his belt line where, down inside his pants, it connected to the crude wooden leg he had worn for so long. In reality, this one was his third, and no lighter than the first. Around the site he looked for Rollie Dobbins, boss man, a little prissy Napoleon had often thought, but more knowledgeable than any man in town on this kind of an excavation. Often enough he'd seen the light go on in Rollie's eyes when a new discovery was made, when a ditch gave up clues or artifacts, when the 17th Century struggled up out of a pile of dirt or the bottom of a hole like a woodchuck checking the lay of the land.

Now, Napoleon had found this new discovery. With effort he tried to reach back into history the way Rollie did. Long had he marveled at how much Rollie could pull out of a small find, the way a rock sat on its neighbor or what it was made of or how the demarcation in a trench of the natural soil line could tell time as good as a calendar.

Napoleon used his head to signal Rollie, as if giving signals to his dog, and nodded to his current digging spot.

Roland Wells Dobbins, dark-haired, round faced, handsome in his ruddy outdoors way, just now beginning to widen at the belt line a bit, tipped dark-rimmed glasses off his face and looked at Napoleon. From long standing he admired the old man, who kept his shovel moving more industriously than any two of the other laborers. Napoleon was also a good luck talisman for Rollie, his charm piece. He remembered the day he had hired the old man, who began methodically shoveling his way through three hundred years of fill. His single eye was a marvelously good organ. A cannon ball popped off his shovel that first day; a half dozen clay pipe remnants (with one bowl intact) turned up an hour later, on the second day the crusted remains of a matchlock pistol were held in the air just as the crew broke for lunch. For that one moment Rollie the archeologist had palmed devilish antiquity.

"What is it, Napoleon?" Sweat was a dark stain on Napoleon's shirt under the one-strap suspender. An off-yellow color it was, almost like an old tobacco stain, and made Rollie think of his grandfather for the first time in many years.

"Where I'm digging, boss. Down where you sent me yesterday to trench out. There's a skeleton." The old man's one eye had a remoteness in it. "It's in the fill. It's in some clay. I don't think I hit it with my shovel, but the front of the skull has been crushed. I didn't tell any of the others. It must have been a nasty death." A story wagged deep behind his one eye, his brow leaning over it darkly.

Rollie looked at his watch, smiled at Napoleon. "Thanks, Napoleon.

Tell the others they can go for lunch. I'll check it out myself." Down the slope Rollie's gait was deliberate, drawing no eyes.

Down into the trench Napoleon had cut he eased himself. A neatness came at him immediately; the floor of the trench was level, the five foot sides were cut down as if they had been carved or sculpted out of the sand and gravel and blue-gray hardpan. The pile thrown out humped a long mound stretching away from the trench. The neat trench itself was about eighteen feet long. Beneath him he saw the bones of the skeleton Napoleon had unearthed. The skull indeed was crushed in at the forehead. Arm bones and torso bones had been exposed. A quick little chill spun on Rollie's skin and danced off someplace. Never before in any of his digs had he seen this. There'd been pots and pans and rocks and stones and clay pipes and glass bottles of every sort and pieces of wood with enough left of their grain that stories could still be extracted from them. But never the hard remains of a human being; just the subtle remains, the storied remains, never the boned and final remains.

The other workers thought it odd that Rollie and Napoleon during lunch had quickly set up a canvas tent over the trench. They hadn't seen a tent on-site in almost a year. It was, obviously, now out of bounds for them.

The third party on the scene, a daily visitor to the site, was Officer Silas Tully of the Saugus Police Department. For a couple of years he had watched as Rollie Dobbins pieced together so much of the original site from piles of rock and slag heaps and baskets full of artifacts, and now wondered what a tent signified. Curious, he made his way down to the tent, stepping over trenches with his long legs, jumping over small piles of slag or rocks, avoiding larger holes and pits. Rollie and he had become, if not friends, at least daily conversationalists on the topic of excavation. Each loved the way details and mysteries worked on them and each found in the other a sense of mirror. The particulars of each calling worked resolutely.

Si Tully slipped aside the canvas door flap of the tent and stepped inside. Rollie looked up at him from the bottom of the trench, a non-plused look on his face as if a policeman was absolutely the last person he wanted on site. With some effort Rollie climbed the ladder out of the trench. Touching the blue sleeve of Silas' shirt, a pained look, as if he had been surprised at the cookie jar or caught peeking in the girl's bathroom, flooded his face. In the hanging light of a Coleman lamp buzzing its ignition as noisy as bees his face reddened deeply.

"Si, we just can't let too many people in on this until we found out what it's all about!" His eyes affected beseeching. "They'll trample the hell out of the place. It'd take us months to recover. We can't let strangers in here."

"Find out what's what all about?" Silas said, and then, swiftly directed, he looked along the length of Rollie's arm pointing at the skull in the bottom of the trench, its forehead obviously crushed at a point of history.

Six years on the force and this was Si Tully's first skull and, moreover, his first skeleton. Bodies he'd seen, that's for sure, in the islands on the turnpike at crash scenes, laid out on the median strips more times than he cared to remember. This, though, was a new mystery to him; an unknown, a victim how long in the historic grave no one knew or might never know. Something told him that Rollie had made assessments, that one or more leads had already surfaced, that this gruesome crime would be solved. It was second nature to the archeologist. This could be most interesting, a bizarre and intriguing find at the archeological site, more than history unfurling itself.

Si spoke again. "It's my town, Rollie, and it's murder clear as a bell, and I've got to report it. You know that. No matter how old it is." The former Marine, the military man, early in this new episode, could see lines being crossed, basic command structure being aborted.

Rollie had seen the quizzical light in Silas' eyes before. Again he touched him on the arm. This time it was as if he were drawing the young policeman into a strictest confidence; the secret of King Tut's tomb, a hidden room beneath the Sphinx, a new Rosetta Stone unearthed in old Yankee Saugus. Consciously he decided not to tell Silas of the other waiting discovery; there were stars to be earned! Treach had paved the way.

Rollie stood beside the trench looking down at the skeleton, down where history was always telling him stories. A storyteller might have been reciting the sad and gruesome tale to him, a tale of love turned sour, of madness, a tale of clandestine deeds performed or perpetrated under cover of darkness. In the air he could feel hatred, and despair. A man, he thought, a seaman perhaps, had come home from the high angry seas only to find more trouble at the hearth. His mind kept telling him it had a will of its own, despite the training, the years of experience. Mystery, he knew, did it. But, he thought with some eagerness, he lived on mysteries.

Robby still held Silas by the arm, working on the mystery, the love of details in the policeman which made his own life go 'round. "I'm going to get Professor Hartley out here from Harvard. Loves this place he does and he'll love this challenge. I can see him marshaling the forces at Harvard, getting his cronies in the labs to do us a few favors. His forensic friends will have a small busman's holiday on this, their own little murder to play with. They'll love it, the boys of the old school, in a deep, dark secret, rolling up their pant legs and getting down and dirty. They'll give us the answer to every question we can come up with, you and I. Then, with it all laid out, you can go to the chief or the State or whoever else and lay a clean solved case right on the blotter." There was affirmation in his eyes, in his voice.

He squeezed Silas' arm. They were standing there on the edge of history. It could have been The Valley of Kings under their feet, or Chichen tza or a Ming Dynasty tomb somewhere in China. Again he squeezed Silas' arm, brothers of the mystery.

Early Sunday morning two station wagons rolled into the parking area of the Iron Works. Rollie and Silas met Professor D'Jana K. Hartley, tall, effectively studious-looking in his tweed leathered elbows, but not in a boring way, and his cohorts from the ivy halls; two more archeologists, a forensic expert and his young sidekick with blond hair and extremely bright eyes, a professor of Humanities who looked to be the most intelligent of all, a man who carried from the trunk of one car a canvas bag of assorted gear, and a young good-looking woman wearing denim, boots and a yellow blouse fitting her so well that most others would not believe she was from Harvard. None of the site diggers, that's for sure, noting how compelling yellow was.

Napoleon deMars watched them approach. Leaning on his shovel near the tent, he was still on the clock, still at $2.35 an hour, and no one, not one soul, had entered the tent since he'd received his orders from Rollie. Perhaps the victim was as old as he was, perhaps a person he had known in his youth. His mind went skipping back through the years for a noted loss. Nothing came to mind. Napoleon watched the Harvards at work and admired the deftness of their hands with the small trowels and brushes they employed, yet was certain the soft leather boots they wore must have cost a week's pay. He tried to hear the whispers and small asides that connected them, made them such outlanders down in the hole he had cut into the earth.

Professor D'Jana Hartley's crew were crack specialists. Quietly they went their turn back into the minor history of the skeleton in the trench of the Iron Works. Small talk amongst them, as much whisper as anything could be, as if covering a trail of a known confidant, had scanned a series of possibilities: an indentured servant, probably a Scot, a slag toter or bog digger or barrow pusher, who had fallen astray, perhaps with another slave's woman or the Iron Master's wife, and they tittered at a remark about a new ax of Cane manufactured on the very spot and which had done the improbable deed; a late visitor to the site, pocketbook or pouch laden with crown coin or Spanish gold pieces, fallen under the swing of a metal bar, come slowly as an ingot of first life out of the very furnace whose ruins lay at their backs, in the hands of another indentured servant waiting to buy his way out of contract.

Now and then a giggle caught itself on the tall air. Napoleon, intently watching every move, hearing every sound, thought of his grandchildren at the cookie jar and smiled at the likeness of things. He'd work till ninety if they let him, and if the other leg would hold its own, here in this affable cradle of history. On the way home he'd buy a box of cookies for the cookie jar; it was a fair swap.

The dig, though, was a Chinese checkerboard of ups and downs, holes and trenches and piles and mounds of earth, almost a battle zone of sorts. The slag pile looked like it might have oozed out of the place where Rollie had said the furnace originally was. It was twenty feet high or thereabouts and ran towards the river for ninety or more feet. When the sun caught a slick side of slag, like a shiny piece of coal with an enamel surface, one would think of a semaphore signal leaping from darkness. The land sloped away from the Iron Master's House on the high point to where the salt water reached at high tide, a good two miles and a half up the Saugus River from the Atlantic Ocean, itself a trove of history. Legend had it that a pirate captain, Treach or Langton perhaps, had brought his ship a good way up the river and then landed a long boat further up, a boat which had carried much of his plunder to be buried in Dungeon Rock, now a huge hole 135 feet down in solid rock and bare miles away in the Lynn Woods Reservation.

The young policeman, at the same time, was not standing still. A minor conviction had told him that the skeleton was not too old; at least, not of Colonial age. This conviction he accepted as coming from an intelligence and a feel for things that he had cultivated while on the job and while in the military. Immediately he had gone to a retired postman, a neighbor of his for years, who was a veritable historian of the town, gossip or rumor or fact. Silas had found out that the stagecoach road from Boston to Newburyport had, at one time, run right past the backside of the Iron Works. That, too, was on what was now Central Street. That Central Street, still clear in Silas' mind, had once swept right on by the front of the Iron Works. Somewhere in town, a long time ago, but not as long as some might think it, a person had disappeared, or had been murdered, or had been buried in the lap of history. Silas Tully made his mind up that he was going to solve this case, that he would find out whose bones had been buried at the Iron Works.

The weekly *Saugus Advertiser* and the *Lynn Daily Evening Item*, Lynn the next town over, seemed to be his best choices and he began a one-man search for a person who had suddenly gone unaccounted for. Through reams and reams of old copies he labored. To old time reporters and editors he talked and in turn haunted the cracker barrels and barroom back rooms and sundry other locations they had directed him to. These were places where history walked, where history talked, where the tongues of history carried on the legends and the lineage that might never make its way into print. Over-the-fence stuff. Dark alley stuff. Stories he never heard before surfaced, debris riding up on the tide, swollen drains dumping pieces of the town into the river, silt of lives streaming away. Old copies of defunct *Saugus Gazette* and *Saugus Herald* and *Lynn Transcript* newspapers brought nothing to light. No headlines, no want ads for a lost person, no missing person with no single accounting. No melodramas in the local library of a missing girl or boy or a triangle affair gone haywire.

But he was resolute.

It was *Ars Veritas* that brought things into focus after Rollie's discovery of the coin.

An informal, unsigned, handwritten report came to Rollie Dobbins a mere three days after the Harvard entourage had first hit the Iron Works. Line by line, item by item, he considered the information set forth:

The subject is male, thirty-one years of age, dead of a savage blow to the frontal lobe of the skull. Death was immediate. It is estimated that he has been covered (Rollie almost giggled at the word) since mid year of 1905. His watch stopped at 2:17 of a day, in the AM we would assume, and was German, a Gersplank, very limited in production and rarely seen this side of the Atlantic. He carried a small sum of coin. One leg, the right, was 3/4 inch shorter than the other. He had been an accident victim prior to his demise, his hip and thigh bone both having been fractured, the right side, and most likely about two years prior to his end. He was perhaps in military uniform at the time of his death, as determined by tunic buttons found at the site, an officer of a captain's rank, United States Cavalry, 22nd Regiment Massachusetts. No military identification was found onsite, which we find questionable and suspicious in nature, inasmuch as his pouch was neither emptied nor removed. Two bones in right index and right middle finger were broken which we assume to have happened at or close to the scene of discovery, at time of death, meaning struggle. A length of chain had been dropped or had fallen onto the body and was found, remains of it, rusted solid on top of the spinal column. No other objects or material were found in proximity of the remains except for a small figure of jade of unknown origin discovered a mere two feet from the left hand, the figure tending towards Chinese but not yet confirmed, but probably pre-Ming.

In summation we offer the following: Victim was a 31 year old professional military man with healed bone fractures of hip and leg and was probably in uniform at death but must have been on a limited duty roster; did struggle at time of death as evidenced by broken fingers but was mortally wounded and died immediately from severe trauma to forehead. May have had Chinese or Far East connection, if indeed the jade piece found nearby does not prove to be Incan or pre-Incan. Our camp is exactly halved on this last point.

The lack of any evidence of fabric, other than his pouch, gathers suspicion the more we have think about it, especially concerning tunic buttons and no tunic residue of note. It is possible that his uniform was biodegradable and has passed on, but we doubt that. Therefore we think he may have been nude (stripped under duress) and pushed bodily into a hole. If he was nude, the evidence of tunic buttons indicates they may have been placed there to mislead any subsequent authority inquest, and we must ask why. Certainly, the person who committed this deed did not expect it to be discovered in the foreseeable future, but was covering tracks for any discovery some years down the road. It therefore causes us to think he was known to the victim, was himself in the military, tried to put sand in the gears (so to speak) (Rollie giggled), or, as D'Jana Hartley said on last resort, it was a military man who killed a civilian and tried to thwart any future identification by throwing in the tunic buttons, like the proverbial hand of gravel as in dust unto dust, probably off his own shirt, a kindly killer who took the shirt off his own back.

We have a world wide network working on the jade figure and feel that it was indeed a portion of loot from some local robbery. We shall keep you advised as to all incoming information or any changes in our collective thinking. In close proximity to the remains was found a 1903 one cent piece, but we do not know if this coin was interred with the remains or had later fallen into the hole during excavation.

Archeologist Rollie Dobbins, giggling at much of the report, finding the humor effective, the conclusions as palpable as his own, and, for the most part, felt the mystery deepen.

Saugus patrolman, and armchair detective when he had to be or needed to be, Silas Tully, at receiving the report and the information on the 1903 cent, found his new starting point and went right to it. For no reason apparent to himself, he gave a grace year to the passage of time, skipped 1904 and went right to 1905. 1905, it appeared, after much scrutinizing of papers and books and magazines and other information almanacs, was the year of the Russias, or, as he quipped to himself, the year the Russias didn't do too well. The Japs whipped their butt all over hell in their war; they lost 200,000 in the Mukden battle alone, had their naval fleet destroyed in the Strait of Tsushima, lost Sakhalin Island outright, got badly overrun in Manchuria, and a number of other places. Crewmen of the great battleship *Potemkin* mutinied and eventually turned the ship over to Rumanian authorities. The Russian Grand Duke, Sergei Aleksandrovich, the uncle of Czar Nicholas II, was assassinated by a bomb thrown into his lap by a revolutionary. The Russian pot certainly was stirring and much of the world was in turmoil, and, of course, he realized, being on this side of the information trail one could see to where a lot of all this was leading.

A few other events attracted his eye, disparate events, no obvious ties between them, but events that rode on top of tidal debris, like cheese boxes or pieces of flotsam, bobbing to be noticed: the Cullinan Diamond, all 3,106 carats of it, was discovered in Transvaal and insurance underwritten by a U.S. company; the body of American Naval hero John Paul Jones was found in a cemetery in Paris and was moved to the United States in a new casket aboard the USS Brooklyn; the Russian-Japanese War was ended by a pact signed practically in Saugus' own back yard, at Portsmouth, New Hampshire, after a key role was played by the old stick-swinger himself, President Teddie Roosevelt, and closer to home, just a few miles away, the palatial home of W. Putnam Wesley, on the Saugus-Wakefield line in what had become the Breakheart Reservation, was robbed in the dead of night by an unknown male who threatened three servants with bodily harm or death if they tried to escape from a pantry they had been locked into, chopping off a butler's finger with an old sword to prove his vow.

Silas Tully went to sleep that night after chewing all these things over in his mind, locked in on all the international stuff, he knew he was out of his element. But down deep something fervent told him he was going along for the whole ride. All the way. And a bare thread of light, the thinnest lisle possible, gossamer at best, seemed to be pulling at these disparate events.

Upon W. Putnam Wesley he settled for his first stepping stone towards a solution. Filthy rich to say the least, much of it come by way of his grandfather from the California gold fields and parlayed by his father, Wesley had various shades of darkness sitting around him. He had journeyed far and wide, especially in Europe and the Far East, often with a large entourage. His interest included, after money, artifacts of historical intrigue (such as dueling swords or dueling pistols from famous encounters), *objects d'art* tending to explicit sex of any selection, gems so special that there might not have been a match with another, all things Chinese that might be described by one or more of the aforementioned. He had had four wives, three of which died in the midst of a long trip or voyage. Silas found one report of his fourth wife having taken a shot at him, in jest as they declared. Silas figured the threat of that single shot to have saved her life.

Wesley was called Puttee from his earliest days, both from his middle name and from his adventurous youthful habit, when playing soldier games, of wearing strips of cloth which circled his legs from ankle to knee, much in the manner of real soldiers. His name he wore well.

The sixth sense was working overtime for Silas a few days later when he sat with Rollie under a tarp at the Iron Works site. They discussed their points of view and all the data of the *Ars Veritas* report.

"It's a crime of passion," Rollie finally affirmed, his voice steady, convincing in its stoic way, his dark serious eyes looking out over the site and seeing, oblivious to Silas Tully, what the site would eventually look like. His baby, Rollie's baby, put to bed.

A marriage is involved," he continued, "a triangle affair. I think we must look to the Hawkridges. Powerful, money by the handfuls, owners of the site for a long time, their papers still scattered throughout the Iron Master's house like they've just gone away for the weekend and will be back on Monday to square things away."

He seemed to mull over his own words before he added, "Perhaps the Hawkridges were so powerful that the absence of one of the family could easily be explained."

"You've found something?" Silas said, turning to face Rollie as they sat on a fence rail. The light in Rollie's eyes was amber, obvious. Silas, from day one of their acquaintance, knew that Rollie's bent was to the romantic, to the clandestine, Rollie's eye having that other light in them.

"Yes," Rollie said. "One of the Hawkridges, Carlton Theophus Hawkridge. About thirty years of age that I know of. Went off on a trip somewhere around 1905, perhaps a bit later, and was never heard from again."

"How do you know that?"

"From a few letters I found in a box in the upper rooms. Went off supposedly very quickly on a trip for his health. Not the most likable fellow, not from what I gather, but *family*."

"Do you think the family did him in?" Si's eyes were deep with question, his scowl like punctuation.

"I really don't know that, but we scrambled at the beginning of all this to go a lot further back than we thought we could. "What have you come up with?"

As though he expected no reply, Rollie looked away from Silas, seeing the sun catch on the water of the river, an angular slicing of light in the late afternoon, sometimes gold, sometimes blue, that leaped across the river and onto Vinegar Hill where he just knew Treach's treasure was buried. The hole being dug he could picture, the chest being lowered, the rocks being piled up. He could see the descent of the crew back down to the longboat, could see their soft and easy float down the river to the ship shifting slightly at anchor. He knew where his next job was coming from. And if the skeleton in the trench was one Carlton Theophus Hawkridge, or could safely assumed to be so, the move to the next dig would be a cinch.

So much depended on the young policeman sitting beside him. Spoon feeding him would be a challenge. Subtle as a snake it would need to be.

Silas Tully gave nothing away. Not even the fact that he knew he was not a rank amateur, that knots in spite of all apparent were being slowly tied, that the gossamer thread would come to rope. If Roland Dobbins had his blind romance, he had his own.

"I just keep poking along, Rollie, trying to tie things together. It's all so far away, as if never touching us with reality."

"If it's Hawkridge, Si, I can see a spread in the Boston papers for you. Perhaps a magazine article. You could turn this old Yankee town right up on its ear! They'll be beating a path to your door. You couldn't beat them off." His smile was broader than a shovel blade. And the shovel blade was slicing deep into a pile of manure.

"The Japanese tried that, Rollie. It didn't work for them either." There was a declaration he hoped Rollie would understand. Edging off the fence rail, he waved slightly, almost half-heartedly. "I'll keep you posted, Rollie. You do the same." There was another one.

As Si walked off, Rollie looked out over the site, saw a glancing shaft of light leap off the river and leap up to the crest of Vinegar Hill. Treach just knew he was coming after him! Bet on it!

The gossamer thickened indeed later that week for Silas Tully.

An article in an old issue of a discontinued Boston paper, about Old Ironsides and the Charlestown Navy Yard, tied together John Paul Jones and W. Putnam "Puttee" Wesley. It was a single line implying that the container bringing home the body of the hero was used to illegally convey some priceless artifacts. And Puttee Wesley was accompanying the body home, a service he so graciously volunteered to perform, inasmuch as he was in Paris and on his way home. President Roosevelt accepted the offer. The thin line of gossamer, with a little more body to it, seemed to fall like a shadow of netting on the piece of jade that had lain so long in the earth beside another body.

Silas had come to abrupt attention, as if the old Commander-in-Chief himself had walked in on him. Life was full of little pieces of goodness. Find them, that's all you had to do. They were at your feet, in your back pocket, around the corner.

Puttee Wesley, he decided from all that he ingested of him, was not afraid of playing either the pirate or the brigand or the smuggler to get any of the items his heart desired. If money wouldn't buy them, he'd get them one way or another. In 1919 he had died suddenly, unprotected by his money or his treasures, from a bout with influenza. The family then, as many families do under pressure, had scattered, their fortunes wasted, and little evidence of Puttee Wesley's existence hung on. Breakheart had become pond and forest and a scattering of trails, the huge mansion gone to ground, a bare bit of stone foundation thrusting out of brush.

But to Silas there came echoes repeating themselves like gunshots down between canyon walls, the continuing onslaught of the same notion. . . all these things, Jones and Puttee and the jade piece and the skeleton, were caught up in the same web, the same gossamer spinning out of his mind, spinning out of the twist of all the years.

Rollie Dobbins had tried to plumb Silas' mind a number of times, tried to steer him to the Hawkridges, but fell short with each attempt. The stubbornness of the young policeman, though a craggy veteran, bothered him more than he let on.

Treach had waited this long, but he might not wait forever. Even in death the pirate might be a most rambunctious ghost.

It took a strange turn of events to swing matters in the correct direction, the kind of luck that Silas Tully knew would come of endless scratching, endless probing, endless digging, his own *l'affair archeology*. If his French were much better he'd be able to spell it right.

It was a naval clerk at the Pentagon who remembered Silas Tully's numerous inquiries about the John Paul Jones transfer, who had seen Silas' letter concerning the suspicions surrounding the hero's remains being brought home, who a long time earlier in his current assignment had begun reading old documents in the Navy archives.

Seaman First Class Peter J. Leone wrote the following to Officer Silas Tully of the Saugus Police Department:

This is not an official document and is only sent to you on a personal basis because of the interest you have excited in me about the Admiral John Paul Jones situation. I have come across a number of old documents and communiqués concerning the Admiral's coming home to where he should have been. If there is anything else I might furnish, I will try, but I think you will be interested in what has caught my eye in the files. The president at the time, Theo. Roosevelt, was advised of certain shady deals that might be attached to the movement of the Admiral's remains. The information came in a letter to him from a Bruce Jacob Bellbend, a captain in British intelligence, who had accidentally come on the information while on a separate assignment. It did mention illegal movement of precious artifacts that had been taken from unknown sources. The president assigned a personal representative, Captain Arthur G. Savage, U.S. Navy, to proceed to Paris and accompany the remains home and to investigate and report to him any and all findings he might come across. None of the captain's reports are in file, but I did find the following information about him: he was from Grand Hawk, Minnesota, was a graduate of the Naval Academy, was captain of the U.S.S. Standish at one time, did suffer a serious accident aboard ship that required medical leave (hip and leg injury in a fall, right side), had a deep scar on his left cheek of unknown cause, was a gutsy and devoted leader of men, and loved nothing better than his country. He was reported as being missing in July of 1905 and nothing more is known of him, as though he had gone off the face of the Earth.

Silas Tully brought his case to rest, though it lay at his feet for a few days, being stepped on, turned over, cemented back into place. He could see Puttee Wesley or one of his henchmen knock the captain on the head, take him under cover of darkness to where Central Street was being filled in, dropping him in the hole, throwing on top of his bare body the buttons of some army tunic to throw leads elsewhere in case the body might be discovered. The jade piece, still unidentified, was sacrificed to help the scattering of leads. The remnants of chain continued to be nothing more than a corrosive coil in his mind. The precious artifacts put away for the time being.

Silas Tully told it all to his wife Phyllis and none of it to Rollie Dobbins.

Napoleon deMars, with the help of two grandchildren and two sons-in-law, held sway over the tent for another week until the remains of the unknown body, as it was officially treated, were laid quietly to further rest in a shaded area of Riverside Cemetery, just outside of Saugus Center, alongside the railroad tracks no longer in use.

One evening thereafter, Rollie Dobbins, maverick archeologist, ramrod of stones and bones, continued to watch the late afternoon sun glance off the river with surprising richness. Flares of light flew like spears, shy sparks reigned as though diamonds had been loosed from chest or pouch. Gallant red wing blackbirds from both sides of the river flew across and through shafts of late light like arrows onto their targets. Dusk, as part of shadow, settled itself softly, a dust, atop the colonial town. Vinegar Hill and Round Hill and Hemlock Hill and Indian Slide and dark passages of Breakheart Reservation shifted into the shadows that history continually lends to its constituents. Treach had such a night, he was sure. And he was out there, his subtle remains, waiting for him in those shadows.

And one night a few weeks later, when all was quiet, the sky a dark canopy, Silas Tully, a policeman always, a Marine forever, a patriot feeling the pains of wounds he had long forgotten, his eyes raw with sadness, thinking of the admiral and the captain and the president and the seaman at the Pentagon, knowing the town he loved would cement the ultimate resolve, affixed above that single grave at the Veteran's Section of Riverside Cemetery a wooden sign he had carved one long night filled with the deepest of thoughts. It read: *ARTHUR G. SAVAGE, CAPTAIN U.S. NAVY, WHO DIED IN THE SERVICE OF HIS COUNTRY.*

There would be no fanfare, no clarions or trumpets or drums. No gunfire. The captain would sift into the past, along with all the other veterans from all the other wars, all the warriors the town had ceded to history. He'd have a flag atop his grave on Memorial Day, put there by the American Legion. The breeze and the sunlight would catch at it, flapping it about. Children would wave back. A few seniors, offering up their own kinds of parades, would offer serious nods. The wind would come back again and again, a rapture of touch, a salute of sorts. Nights would accept the continual silence abounding in Riverside.

Silas Tully thought he could give Captain Arthur Savage nothing more precious than that.

When he told his wife, she loved him all over again.

Reverse Triggers

A woman who long ago lived below us, a single mother of one, once found an unfamiliar folder hidden away in the program files of her family computer. Inside were photos of her daughter, arranged and labeled by weight—*111 lbs., 104 lbs., 92 lbs.*—along with assorted pictures of runway celebrities collected from entertainment sites and before-and-after photos of other teens, friends the girl made through online *thinspiration* forums and chat rooms, labeled as low as 63 lbs. And there were other images—reverse triggers, her daughter calls them—of pregnant women and the grossly obese.

After, when she searched her daughters room, she found the jars of vomit in the closet, the diet pills in the drawer, and the misspelled entries in her daughters diary journaling her food intake:

Breakfast:
Three cigaretes. Two cups coffee. Water.

Lunch:
Sugarless gum—half a pack. Jello—two cups. Skimmed milk. Frosting from one cupcake.

Breakfast:
Four cigaretes. No coffee. Half bag Doritos.

She read on, finding other entries graphing weight changes, expressing the geeniusness of eating ice cubes and lollypops for dinner, and quoting the morbidly misunderstood conceptions of historys finest:

"We never repent of having eaten too little."
Jefferson

"Things sweet to taste prove in digestion sour."
Shakespeare

"Quod me nutrit me destruit" (What nourishes me destroys me)
Angelina Jolie

The woman realized then how little she knew her daughter. She confronted the girl, who denied and cried and retreated to the bathroom to calm her nerves in bubble bath—and later, when her mother returned to try again, failed to answer from behind the bathroom door. The woman assumed the worst, popped the lock with a bobby pin, and found her daughter in the tub, wrists sliced with a bread knife and sticky with blood. She pulled her out through the hot and pink bubbles to find that her daughter was fully dressed—a hooded sweatshirt and jeans, the cotton waterlogged and steaming—and that she was several pints lighter.

Her mother's blood saved the girl, and afterwards she found help: group therapy, psychiatrists, inpatient facilities. And years later the girl was happy and plump, tattoos of butterflies over each of her scars: a Cranberry Blue on her left—*Vacciniina optilete*—a Mourning Cloak on her right—*Nymphalis antiopa*—the raised and jagged cut marks hidden in the veins of blue and black wings, imperceptible to all but the two who know them best.

But the single mother of one saved the photos from the hidden folder she found in the program files of the family computer, and she kept them as reminders—reverse triggers, things to be happy for—changing only the file names, replacing the churlish weights with random letters: *asjkl. jkljp. dsagdu. tyadsj. risjdf. iosdgj.*

The Broken House of Nanjing

D r. Jian Hsing, a Chinese professor of history, used to sit out on his back deck in the morning light and work on his manuscript, a memoir about growing up in Nanjing decades after the massacre. He'd sift through photos of disemboweled women, young girls bayoneted through lower orifices, charred bodies left without remorse, and he'd read through transcripts of an American reporter who described the streets so strewn with bodies that one had no choice but to drive over them to reach the safety zone; an interview with a woman who survived days of near-constant gang rape and nearly a dozen bayonets through her chest and neck before being found, nearly lifeless, by passersby and nursed back to a state of health checked by scars, disability, and venereal disease.

When he was finished with his fourth draft and sitting on a growing pile of rejection letters he asked the administration if he could read a chapter in the central quad, and they set up a podium twenty yards from a group of sorority girls selling raffle tickets for an all expense paid trip to Cabo. But few looked and fewer listened. The sorority girls' solicitous screams drowned out talk of rape and mutilation and Japanese denial and omission from history books, and a circle of friends joked behind cigarettes while cell-phoned students crossed the professor's back and front on their way to class.

The professor returned home and fell into a depression. He stopped going to work. Stopped going anywhere. And several weeks later, when his neighbors mailed him a letter asking him to mow his lawn, he responded by distributing his collection of transcribed notes and post-mortem photographs to their mailboxes. When they didn't respond he distributed the full manuscript, and when they mailed a second letter informing him that his use of their mailboxes was a violation of federal law and asking him to please mow his lawn, the professor took a machete to his bushes, a hammer to his mailbox, rocks to his windows, and a crowbar to his roof—where he lost his footing trying to peel up shingles, and fell beside his mutilated bushes.

He came back from the ER with a line of stitches, a concussion, and a leg cast—but not before making friends with the physician who treated him: a Japanese man called Chiyuu whose wife, Susan, a fledgling assistant at a New York publishing house, got her first break weeks later with the acquisition of Jian Hsing's memoir: "The Broken House of Nanjing."

Everything

S he raises her hands and covers her closed eyes with them. Tries not to think of anything. When she presses the fingertips tight against her lids, it arrives, magically. Phosphene. This she knows about. This she can think about. And when it fades into something else, she feels a sense of arrival. She lives for journeys.

What is within her sight interests her now. In her sight, so delicately held by her fingertips, there is a house, an aged white clapboard. Maybe the house is in Maine or Massachusetts, but she cannot be sure of this. Quickly, she needs to know what surrounds the old house. Some trees, to be sure. Perhaps a pond, frozen or not. What fascinates her most is the lawn that surrounds the house.

The lawn is full of clouds. All shapes and colors. The clouds are drifting, carrying the house along. Another journey. Through space. Then, on the clouds, a boy appears. Maybe fifteen years old, and nude. Longish brown hair. He is walking through the clouds. She knows him, has seen him before, always walking. She even has a name for him. Tim. He walks through the clouds and never seems to stop for rest. A sky pilgrim.

He exists for her alone. If she takes her fingertips from her eyes, he's gone. The house disappears. Clouds drift up and away. Whatever was there must wait for her, for another chance. It's up to her. Her touch. Everything depends on this.

Happy Jack's Glorious 40 Minutes

Minutes 0–20

The Tampa Bay Ice Palace lay off to his left, across the road, now darkened by the bedding of the sun. Happy Jack popped his last ecstasy tab, took a swig from the Pepsi bottle he'd just bought at the 7/11, and let out a satisfying belch. His third tab in two hours and the effect was starting to get really strange. The emporium, in his vision, was tantalisingly stark and near.

He moved across the road, dodging the dwindling traffic flow, though not entirely successful as the Nissan Primera failed to swerve and ran over his toes. The drivers' "fucken idjut" was soon lost as the car sped away. Happy Jack looked down then at his right hand and marvelled at how the snub nose 38 Special had dropped into his palm, and realised the concern on the driver's face was due to his amazing reaction. The craziness of the situation forced a demonic laugh from his ecstasy laden lips, soon replaced by the sight of other dark objects flying past him, each showing clearly two moons of their headlights.

His foot hurt, hurt like hell, but his renewed vision of the stadium drew him forward in his purpose. He could hear it, the sound from within, and the thump of the bass drawing him ever onwards.

. . . .It all makes perfect sense. . . .
. . . expressed in dollars and cents,
pounds shillings and pence. . . .

Roger Waters stood on the stage, staring down at the less than impressive opening night crowd. The bastards were giving him a grilling, moving around; shouting out the obscene "Pink Floyd" chant that really pissed him off, and those bloody pinpoints of laser light were giving him a grating migraine.

. . . . can't you see. . . .
it all makes perfect sense. . . .

Roger looked over to Doyle Bramhall II, who appeared to be lost in the moment of trying to perfect every note, to keep the fans from complaining. Roger marvelled at the ease with which the young guitarist could hit the notes, the smoothness of the style. Damn, if he wasn't another guitarist from long ago. Thank god he wasn't a waster though. Never again, thought Roger.

"Thank you everybody, it is magic here tonight. . . ." Roger hated saying the words as soon as he spoke them. Sure, some in the crowd were appreciative but the rest just carried on with the tirades, the ignorant catcalls. Certainly, he felt happy that he was touring again; trying to connect with the fans, but this first night was just getting too much.

Happy Jack leaned against the wall, pulled out his crumpled packet of Marlboro's, flipped a distorted durrie into his mouth, and flicked his well worn US Navy Seals Zippo into life. He snapped the cover back on, and allowed the fulfilling nicotine to settle into his cavernous lungs. A racking cough erupted forcefully, causing him to bend over and exude the brown phlegm from his throat. After the fit had caused his drug effected heart rate to settle a little, he stood and cleared the rest of the gooey stuff from his mouth and around his chin, wiping it on the back of his fingerless, gloved hand. Hell these things hurt, hurt the cancer in his dying lungs, the agony of the pain stretching into his cancer riddled liver, causing excruciating pain to shoot up his right side. The ecstasy helped to numb it a bit, but still the pain bit.

Roger walked back over to the microphone. The crowd was getting up and starting to walk towards the door, but not all of them. Thank god for that small mercy, at least.

"Ladies and gentlemen, I would like to finish. . . . . . ." The song rolled out and the band hit all the notes to perfection. Damn, the months sequestered away in the recording studio had certainly been well worth it. The sound was meatier, and the song fuller in complexity and the band just nailed it. Roger was pleased.

God stood atop the back row, smiling approvingly at Waters' rendition of Each Small Candle. He was pleased the artiste had chosen to finish with that particular song, but was still mystified at why he had played What God Wants during the show? He knew the song wasn't directly aimed at him, but heavens, it irked to be questioned, and he couldn't help but take it personally. He knew that his mission here was most urgent, but first the people must have their moment. And he knew he had to keep an eye out for Lucifer. Galadriel had mentioned that there was to be a visit tonight, and God had no idea why. He had said that it was a rumour, but the timing was too coincidental.

". . . .*each small candle,*
lights a corner of the dark. . . ."

Happy Jack was swaying to the music, the drug now fully in control, his eyes tight shut to the wondrous sounds of the Greatest Living Anthropologist of the 20th Century. The sound of voices, drunken shouts from his right brought him to erect preparedness. "What the fuck was going on?" he thought. Where did these people come from? A young girl dressed in a miniskirt, high boots and a tight T shirt to accentuate her too large chest, staggered past, giggling her head off, her companion beside her obviously in the same or worse state. He let rip a beer stained belch, which had both of them going off in fits of laughter again.

".... didn't see fucken Dave Gilmour again man," said the oaf, "must've left Floyd again eh, urp......."

"....nuh ya dumb oaf, he quit ages ago, that's why they play shit......"

Their voices trailed away, only to be replaced by more and more as the stadium spilled its dissatisfied Floyd fans.

Happy Jack smiled. They were still ignorant, twenty five years on. He remembered back to his heyday, when he was a Navy Seal moonlighting as a roadie on The Wall concerts, to earn a few more bucks for his cocaine habit. He could have done anything else, he knew, made bigger money doing other clandestine things. But hey, his brother's wife was friends with Terry Lee from the Light and Sound Ensemble, the guys doing the lighting for the show, and being a Pink fan from way back, the opportunity was just two good for Happy Jack to miss. Shit, what an amazing time that was!

But the crowd exodus was rapidly gaining in size, the disaffected leaving in their droves, and inside the auditorium, Roger and the band played on. He withdrew the spent smoke from his lips and flicked it into the path of a passing couple.

"Hey watch it buddy!" the character shouted as the butt hit his face. The black wig became disentangled from the guys' head and fell to the ground revealing a shock of gray-white hair. The fat faced blonde, also obviously wearing a wig, bent down and uttered "don't worry Beelly boy, I'll get it for yo" to which the rather happy and slightly high elderly guy replied "sho Honey, and while you're down there, show us your moniker" and he ripped into peels of laughter.

The bint picked up the wig and spied Happy Jack looking at her. Then she saw the black hole of the 38 pointing straight at her head, and in a wave of panic, pulled the old guy from the direction of the barrel and ran off down the road.

"Moniker, honey, wadda ah say, honey, aw come on honey, He-lary will never know...."

Happy Jack settled back into the shadows, trying hard to soothe his heavy panic stricken breathing. The gun had reacted the same way again, forcing its way into his right hand at the threat of command on his person. 'Shit, shit, shit, I had the perfect chance,' he thought. The President of the United States of America! But he refocused his attention through the haze, on the reason he was here, and it certainly wasn't some dope smoking politician from Arkansas.

Lucifer walked behind the stage, his eyes fixed on the figure atop the stadium seats at the back. It was obvious that God hadn't seen him yet, but soon he must reveal himself, and the battle would then be on. Bloody hell! How he hated that lovey dovey song.

". . . .lights a corner of the dark. . . ."

Lucifer was determined the dark would remain as such.

The music inside the Ice Palace stopped. Applause rang out.

As the crowd started to file out of the main doors, the figure in the park across the road remained impassive, watching the ex-Seal like a hawk, his eyes never leaving the weaving assassin.

Minutes 21–39

Where the hell was the bloody pig? Happy Jack searched the auditorium high and low, emptied now but for the cleaning crews, the roadies securing the stage and a few admin types running around checking for damage. Happy Jack knew there wouldn't be any damage, there never was at a Roger Show. But it didn't help calm his nervousness though. There was always a pig somewhere in the show, but he couldn't for the life him find it anywhere. He thought perhaps his mind was so fucked up from the years of drug abuse that he wasn't registering that pigs' shape anymore. He looked up towards the back of the place and saw God walking down the aisle towards the stage. He was glad he was here. He knew God, had known him for years, since the heroin overdose he and his Seal buddies had been forced to take when captured by the Contra's in South America.

Scary days, then! Eating wild pork with the local tribes, only to be laced and left for dead. But God had come to save him, and pulled him through his crises. But the price had been heavy. The cancer riddling his body was a legacy of those days, those uncaring excursions of youthful exuberance. God had said sorry then but there was nothing he could change about the way he fated his souls.

"Hi again, Happy Jack, hanging in there?" said the entity as he wafted past the bemused hunter. Happy Jack turned and watched him walk up to the side of the stage, the cleaners oblivious to his presence.

'Yeah, bloody fine, thanks' he thought to himself, half-wondering why he had replied. God knew his thoughts anyway, which created another dilemma in his fogged mind. 'Shit, why didn't he stop me from my errand?' He knows what I want to do but he didn't stop me? Happy Jack slumped in one of the seats and stared mindlessly towards the stage, absolute confusion ruling his mind. Where was that damned pig and why didn't God stop me?

"Thanks guys, that was bloody magic. Can't express how much I enjoyed the experience tonight, and don't worry about the crowd, they had big night nerves as well and things will improve, believe me." Roger stood facing the band in the conference room, as each tucked into the after gig fare and drinks, soaking up their maestro's appreciation of their individual efforts. A warm glow emanated from each as they soaked in the glory of the evening.

The dark figure appeared from behind a screen, his coal black eyes covered by an expensive pair of RayBans transfixed on the crowd of musicians, singers, Ice Palace employees, and media especially invited to attend. He was ready to start what had to be done. But he was unnerved. There was a feeling in this room he abhorred. The warmth and love that only satisfied humans could enjoy. His desire was to be sated but the strength of the enemy would be greater for the love in this place.

Dale and Emily danced through the auditorium, Dale resplendent in his nice new blue-gray suit and Emily in her bright purple and pink summer frock, legacies of their 5th birthday party being held next door at the Wendy's restaurant; their parents oblivious to the situation their children found themselves in.

The two children had sneaked out from the playground when they saw all the happy people leaving the Ice Palace, and their curiosity was tickled as to why so many big people were leaving such a large place with very big smiles on their faces. There must be a circus or something going on for everyone to be happy. When they entered the auditorium, they were at first dismayed not to find a circus, but grew inquisitive as to why such a big place was suddenly empty and dreary, yet a moment ago a place of happiness. They started to search the stadium, twins in simpatico, thought patterns reacting to each other's will as if by instinct. They shied away from the area the ugly sad looking man sat, his eyes transfixed on the front of the stage, not seeing the two of them. But they continued up to the back and then back to the front, each descending on opposite sides and racing each other to the stage.

A cleaner tried to shoo them, but gave up when he saw their happy faces. God, by now up on the stage and making for the back stage area, turned and looked at the both of them. The two children recognised him and smiled wanfully, suddenly stopped in their tracks by his presence. God smiled again at them and disappeared behind the curtain. Dale and Emily looked at each other and were somewhat confused.

"Was dat God, Emily?" asked Dale. "He looked like him, eh!"

Emily turned and shook her head in confused agreement, and looked back at the sudden sound from over her left shoulder. The fear in her eyes drew Dale round and then the screaming started.

The 38 slipped magically into his hand again. Happy Jack looked down and couldn't understand what had happened. He looked around and only saw the cleaner and the two children by the stage. He was suddenly very nervous. What had happened to cause the gun to be prepared for action? The cleaner, though somewhat a weird looking dude, didn't display signs of command, and the two kids certainly weren't a threat. He scanned the room but couldn't see a goddam thing that would be considered a demand on his presence. The panic started to rise in his groin, up through his chest, and spread into the paranoia of his mind. Forces he had no idea of how to control reached into the miasma of his brain, grabbing his soul and launching him on his path of destiny.

He rose from his chair, and started running, running and screaming towards the stage, "aaaggggrrrrrrhhhhhhhhhhh" as he passed the two startled children and leapt onto the platform, and through the backstage curtain, following the path that God had taken. He cocked the 38!

Doyle sat by the bar, his strained eyes concentrating on the figure that had entered the room behind Roger. The white symbolic attire the tall dude wore was somehow beautiful and the song started to take form in his mind. The figure sort of looked like his vision of Gandalf the Great from the Lord of the Rings; only this guy seemed more majestic and pure. He shifted his eyes to the right of Roger and saw the other guy that he had noticed before, the one with the RayBans. Man, this guy was the complete opposite to the other, dressed completely in black, with his long flowing shiny-black hair tied up behind him by a red ribbon. He too, bespoke power but a power that was not very healthy, or so he, Doyle, thought. Then he realised it. Right and Wrong! Damn, what is happening. . . . . . .

"Hey you guys, how would you like to jam for a bit?" Jim Carin raised his head from the laptop and addressed the rest of the entourage. "I've just hooked into the BBS, Rog, and that guy Mark Q Warren, you know? He goes by the name of Andersoncouncil, with the West Coast band Daves Rope Swing!" Roger nods at the familiarity of the name and moves over towards the keyboard player. "He's posted a new song and it looks very cool, something we could have a go at."

Dale and Emily watch the cleaner, suddenly aware he is not cleaning anything, but watching them and the strange army guy with the gun. He seems funny, and both telepath the Cat in the Hat to each other. They give a small childishly innocent giggle and turn back to Old Pink, who'd followed the assassin into the arena.

"Hey, mister, are you the Cat in the Hat?" yelled Dale.

The man looked at them, a blank look of deep mystery etched on his unresponsive features. His nose was different; they saw, not that of a cat, but almost like that of the third little pig from their favourite nursery rhyme.

Old Pink looked at the two lovely children. He started the rhyme as if by magic, transfixing the kids with his words.

"Hey Riddle, Diddle,
Two kids in the middle,
I'll see you on the Dark Side of the Moon
When two, Right and Wrong,
and one who writes songs,
face the madman and futures boon."

The kids followed him then as he walked up the stairs to the stage, mesmerised by the words but unsure as to their meaning. Old Pink followed the path of God, and Lucifer before him, and the recent careening crusade of the assassin. The twins followed him, unsure of their destiny but certain it lay in the path they now took. There was no turning back for any of them.

Roger's voice rose over the strumming of Doyle and Snowy's acoustic guitars.

. . . wonder why I write like this
I'm just a product of societies lie
My life seems to run in circles, but
Wherever they run. . . . . .

God and Lucifer were transfixed by the moment, as was everyone in the room. . . .

. . . . make me act like that
You society—made me mad
And you society make . . . .

The girls started to improvise a backing vocal, humming a thread similar to the male voice choir on The Tide Is Turning. . . .

. . . . . . .your head!! Don't listen to me
A madman lurks inside
Seeking relief from this thirst for freedom
Only then will I stand . . . .

Happy Jack burst into the room and pointed the gun at the first figure he saw through the frosted vision of his ecstasy high, and realised very quickly that his aim on God's back wasn't very prudent. He swung the gun to the left on the figure wearing the RayBans, only to feel a deep dread appear in his psyche. . . .

. . . . you say, FIGHT For what you believe
you say but don't fight me or you'll bleed
you say killing a man is not RIGHT!
Then you say take this gun and fight, ...

Old pink strolled in behind Happy Jack, placed an arm around his shoulders and coerced the gun from his grasp by sheer will, forcing the demented drug addict to absolute calm before he was exposed to the crowd happily jamming in the room. . . . . . .
Rogers' voice reached a screaming pleading pitch as he continued the song off the laptop. . . . . . .

You tell me to act normal
But I never understood the rules
Society lives by a double standard
The poor are castaway, the rich are . . . .

The kids wandered in and stood amazed at how so many people could possibly fit into such a small room. Their gaze is stopped rigid on the old guy singing in the middle of the room, a sudden glow warming in their hearts.

. . . . must listen to what I say
Or you yourselves will cast you away
yes we must change or we will die!
Change is THE power you can't deny!!

. . . wonder why I write like this
I'm just a product of societies lie
My life seems to run in circles, but
Wherever they run. . . . . .

God and Lucifer were transfixed by the moment, as was everyone in the room. . . .

. . . . make me act like that
You society—made me mad
And you society make . . . .

The girls started to improvise a backing vocal, humming a thread similar to the male voice choir on The Tide Is Turning. . . .

. . . . . . .your head!! Don't listen to me
A madman lurks inside
Seeking relief from this thirst for freedom
Only then will I stand . . . .

Happy Jack burst into the room and pointed the gun at the first figure he saw through the frosted vision of his ecstasy high, and realised very quickly that his aim on God's back wasn't very prudent. He swung the gun to the left on the figure wearing the RayBans, only to feel a deep dread appear in his psyche. . . .

. . . . you say, FIGHT For what you believe
you say but don't fight me or you'll bleed
you say killing a man is not RIGHT!
Then you say take this gun and fight, ...

Old pink strolled in behind Happy Jack, placed an arm around his shoulders and coerced the gun from his grasp by sheer will, forcing the demented drug addict to absolute calm before he was exposed to the crowd happily jamming in the room. . . . . . .
Rogers' voice reached a screaming pleading pitch as he continued the song off the laptop. . . . . . .

You tell me to act normal
But I never understood the rules
Society lives by a double standard
The poor are castaway, the rich are . . . .

The kids wandered in and stood amazed at how so many people could possibly fit into such a small room. Their gaze is stopped rigid on the old guy singing in the middle of the room, a sudden glow warming in their hearts.

. . . . must listen to what I say
Or you yourselves will cast you away
yes we must change or we will die!
Change is THE power you can't deny!!

The sudden applause rocks the room and Roger and the guitarists look at each other and at Carin.
"Christ, what a great song," called Roger, "what a fabulous anthem."

"Hey, excuse me," called out Dale, "but my Dad told me never to swear in Gods presence."

Everyone turned then towards the small boy and girl standing by the door, holding hands and looking at all the grown ups with childish innocence. Then someone saw the cleaner with the gun, and started to scream. The rest of the crowd started to react, God reached out for the throng to calm the crowd, Lucifer screamed as loud as the rest creating even more mayhem, and Happy Jack's soul reached out for something he couldn't see.

"Stop it!!" yelled Old Pink with controlled strength. Happy Jack immediately looked down at his right hand searching for the gun, and felt the despair when seeing it wasn't there anymore. Lucifer cowered and God took a respectful pace back.

The sudden applause rocks the room and Roger and the guitarists look at each other and at Carin.

"Christ, what a great song," called Roger, "what a fabulous anthem."

"Hey, excuse me," called out Dale, "but my Dad told me never to swear in Gods presence."

Everyone turned then towards the small boy and girl standing by the door, holding hands and looking at all the grown ups with childish innocence. Then someone saw the cleaner with the gun, and started to scream. The rest of the crowd started to react, God reached out for the throng to calm the crowd, Lucifer screamed as loud as the rest creating even more mayhem, and Happy Jack's soul reached out for something he couldn't see.

"Stop it!!" yelled Old Pink with controlled strength. Happy Jack immediately looked down at his right hand searching for the gun, and felt the despair when seeing it wasn't there anymore. Lucifer cowered and God took a respectful pace back.

"What is going on here, please?" Roger asked. "Who are all you people and what are you doing at my bash?"

The two children stepped forward, without a sign of fear on their faces.

Dale pointed to Happy Jack. "Who are you, mister?"

Happy Jack lifted his eyes from his missing gun, and stared at the kid. What had that kid just asked him? Oh, yeah!

"Me, Oh, I'm Happy Jack. I guess I'm the American Dream, defender of the Faith, One of the Brave, and now a sign of the drugged out, the lost and forgotten. Yeah, that's who I am." He dropped his head in sad contemplation.

Emily pointed at Roger. "Who are you, mister?"

Roger looked at the girl with wistful admiration. The strength she and her brother displayed were marvellous to behold in such so young.

"I am the troubadour, the recorder of life, the questioner of old times forgotten, I am the hope of the Now Generation."

The two kids swung their gaze towards God and Lucifer, who both turned towards each other and without saying a word, shook each others hands as if empowered by some greater force to do so. They then disappeared in a blinding light, shaking the already bemused occupants of the room, who were plenty badly shaken by the events thus far.

Old Pink then turned to the children and asked them:

"And children who are you?"

Emily and Dale looked at each other, smiled and lifted their heads high and scanned everyone in the room, looking each in the eye.

"We are the children of your future, the hope, the learners of mistakes, the changers of the ills, the forgivers of the forgotten. We are our parents love, and we are the holders of the candles for the life that is to come." At that message, their eyes rested on Roger Waters, and he felt an empathy that he had striven for, for years.

Minute 40

Emily and Dale returned to their Mum and Dad, still sitting in Wendy's, thinking their two five year old darlings have been in the takeout's playground. Everyone smiles at each other, and exchange family platitudes. However, the warmth of the family is now an encouraging glow and the world changes a bit tonight.

Old Pink fades off into the distant, wondering the thoughts of a happy muse.

Happy Jack strolled through the transfixed assemblage, making a demanding beeline for the laptop on the other side of the room. He brushed Carin aside and read the words displayed on the screen.

The Gunner's Dream "Two Thousand Years" 6/13/00

I sit upon the beach,
staring out
upon the sea,
the tears of sadness rushing in
and washing
over me,
my memories stained
from years of strain
and pouring out in tears,
what have we humans done,
I wonder,

in the last two thousand years.

Two Thousand years of fighting,
Two Thousand years of death,
Too many soulful people
who drew their final breath,
Too many loveless children,
Too many sad old folks,
Two thousand years of wasted lives,
Too many hearts that broke.

As clouds roll in
and gray my thoughts,
I think of all that sin,
that may have been
why we were taught
to think of thee within,
they try to wash away the gold,
the bright light
of the sun,
But without love,
and God above,
I am the lonely one.

Two Thousand years of misery,
Two Thousand years of pain,
Too many innocent children
being sold down the drain,
Too many heartless tyrants,
Too many wounded prides,
Two thousand years of anguish,
Too many wounded cries.
I look out on the sea
before me,
the rising of the waves,
and try to seek a vision
of the ones that
I can save,
The clouds begin to part again,
The sun, it shines
on through,
a prod in my direction
show me what to do?

Two Thousand candles to be lit,
Two Thousand years away,
To make the smallest changes
I have to make them pay,
To seek a path of love and hope,
To reach for souls so pure,
To spread the message far and wide,
To make their lives endure.

I sit upon the beach once more,
staring out
upon the sea,
the waves of gladness rolling in
and breaking
over me,
my memories clear
I have no fear
My heart is full of cheer,
what can we humans do,
I think,
in the next two thousand years

"For Serena. . . ."

Happy Jack, smiles, the first time for nearly twenty years. The pain in his lungs and liver no longer cause him distress and an arm reaches around his shoulders and gives him a bear hug, the warmth and love there for all to see.

"Don't worry, soldier, there is hope for us all yet, even you." Roger is smiling too.

Non-Fiction

Airplanes

I drive my dad to the National Air and Space Museum and stop at the curb under a wheel chair symbol. My dad's new walker is folded in my trunk. It rolls on wheels and he can "brake" it with his handlebars and sit on its red plastic bench. At six feet tall, he is now roughly one hundred and forty pounds. His khaki pants hang on him. The belt he uses has an extra hole he has punched into it himself.

He has grown frail since we jitterbugged to Glenn Miller's *In the Mood* at his eightieth birthday party. A stroke and the years in an independent living facility have weakened him.

My earliest memory goes back more than half a century. I am sitting on a blanket on the beach at the end of our street in Marblehead, Massachusetts. I am not fond of sand, the gritty grains scratched. I wouldn't sit on the blanket until it had been brushed clean and then I wouldn't crawl off of it.

"Hello-o-o-o, Tweetie!" my dad strolls toward the blanket and a feeling of elation comes over me. The image in my memory is short; a second or two. I lift my arms up for him, whining in that familiar baby grunt, "uh, uh, uh!" But my memory ends after that. He is strolling up to me, smiling and I am reaching up to him.

Now he has wandered off before I can park the car and catch up to him. He has entered the wrong door to the Air and Space Museum, but the guards only stop me—gently—directing me to the security folks who need to look through my purse. When I retrieve my purse, I turn to look for my dad. I feel as though I have a child with me and I am reminded of the exhaustion of trying to keep track of my daughter when she was small.

My dad has stopped to look for me. He is bent over his handlebars, squinting behind his glasses. "What took you so long?" he asks.

The moment is bitter. I look into his aquamarine eyes and I want to remind him that I've driven two hours to see him. But I don't. I try to think of what it must feel like to be facing the last years of your life, to have lost the control you once had over everything, including the airplane that is suspended behind him.

The shock of my father's decline is never softened. Every time I see him, I am reminded of how different he is now. He has become indignant as he's grown old.

I remember I was furious at him for canceling a carefully planned trip to Chincoteague Island the morning we were to go. He spoke in short, angry sentences as he explained that he'd fallen on his way to the bathroom in the middle of the night. He couldn't spend a week on a "remote" island. He was given a clean bill of health later that day, but the trip was off, and he was as irate with me because the trip had to be canceled as he was with himself for calling it off.

Dad would ride bicycles with me. We'd ski and ice skate together and he taught me how to jitterbug. He was fond of big band music and never missed the annual father-daughter dance at my college.

Dad had a light touch and he would bite his tongue as he concentrated on our dance steps. He'd twirl me out from our embrace and fold me back into it, walking beside me a few steps. Then, he'd pat me on the back lightly and twirl me out again, singing a few words with the music: "... *years have gone by... my, my how she grew...* "

Once, he'd told me about a big band singer he knew. He'd met her on leave in California during World War II. I'm fairly certain my mother never knew about her.

Dad sits on his walker's bench, in front of the plane he flew in World War II and I snap a photo of him. The grayish blue Corsair F4U hangs from the ceiling and dips toward him.

I remember taking another picture of him in the cockpit of a Corsair at an air show more than a dozen years ago. My daughter was small and impatient, she told me she didn't want to "look at a bunch of old planes." But my father was a celebrity that day.

He was not only allowed access to the cockpit, he was also invited into the pilots' tent to talk about his experiences. I took my daughter to look for ice cream and left him with the veterans from wars decades after World War II, to discuss the smell of raw gas in the cockpit, the sticky sweat of a flight suit and ill fitting flight masks.

(I knew the story of my dad plucking the wrong mask in a rush to get in the sky. He lost the feeling in his upper lip. All my life, my mother or I would tell him to wipe off the food he sometimes left on his mouth.)

Dad was eighteen years old when the Japanese bombed Pearl Harbor and the United States needed pilots. He went through an accelerated training program at the Massachusetts Institute of Technology. His aviator classmates were all about the same age and it was the first time that M.I.T. accepted men from the armed services.

He would tell me about the M.I.T. dean of advanced aeronautical engineering who wrote what looked like mathematical formulas on the blackboard as he and about forty-five others took their seats. Three walls of the room were covered in blackboards, and the professor wrote on all three, filling them up. When he finished and turned around to look at the class, he dropped the chalk and picked up a ruler. The professor asked for a show of hands for everyone who had a degree in aeronautical engineering. My dad and the others looked at one another. No hands went up. The professor asked for a show of hands for anyone with a college degree. One hand was raised. Finally, the professor asked how many had graduated from high school. Instantly, every hand shot up in the air.

"My. My."

My dad would imitate the way the professor looked around the room, tapping the ruler against his chin. Then, he went to the blackboards and erased everything he'd written on them.

Today, a couple watches us as I take my dad's picture and asks him if he flew the airplane. My dad tells them that he provided close air support for the troops on the ground in a Corsair just like that one.

The man smiles, nods and shakes my dad's hand, "Thank you for your service."

My dad beams, turns to me and says, "Let's go see it from the ground floor."

We start down the ramp of the large hangar; it is located near Dulles Airport. When this extension to the National Air and Space Museum opened, my dad walked through it on his own steam. We talk of the museum's donor, Steven F. Udvar-Hazy. Neither of us knows who he is, but my dad is delighted that he helped make these additional displays possible. Dad wants to see the *Enola Gay*, which is parked on the ground floor around the corner from where his Corsair hangs. The World War II bomber dropped the first atomic bomb on Hiroshima, Japan.

My dad was grinning when he sang, "*. . . on my back at thirty thou if my engine conks out now. . .*"

We were flying over Lake Winnipesaukee, New Hampshire in my uncle's sea plane. My father was at the controls, and the plane was loud. Houses with screen porches peeked out from the green bursts of foliage. Long wood planked piers jutted into the lake and the sun sparkled like shiny coins on the gray/blue water. I focused on the ripple of waves as we got closer and closer, splashing down and taxiing to my aunt and uncle's house. The hangar for their plane was next to it, like a huge garage that opened to the water. It had green aluminum sides. That was the only time I ever flew with my dad at the controls and I felt his excitement. Joy emanated from him.

Halfway down the ramp at the air museum, we stop to rest. People pass us. A man in a Red Sox baseball cap with two women—one in a sari, the other in a long sleeved tunic—following him. The women wear elaborate sandals, forcing them to take small, careful steps. Two men, probably father and son, walk with their eyes focused on something just beyond my dad. I follow their gaze; a small plane, suspended from the ceiling, that looks like a toy. The older man, with curly silver hair, says, "Look at that! A scientific sample collector!" "Ok, let's go," Dad says, rising from his bench where he has parked halfway down the ramp. We turn to descent the rest of the way to the bottom floor, walking parallel to the first part of the ramp that connects to the top floor.

A crowd of about twenty has gathered beneath the Corsair and my dad pushes his walker as close to the guide as he can, scowling while he listens.

I don't pay attention to the guide's words, though I do hear "World War II" as I watch my dad.

Touching the guide's arm when he stops talking, I say, "Sir, here is one of the pilots of that plane."

"What?" the man looks at me. His name tag reads, "Lee." He is in a summer tweed sports jacket; beige. Aviator eyeglasses. Handsome, and younger than my dad by maybe a decade. A big grin breaks out on his face and his perfect teeth, slightly yellow, appear between his parted lips. "Is that right? You flew that plane?"

My dad nods his head, pushes his walker up to Lee. "Yes, that's right. I did." He speaks clearly, better than I've heard him talk in a long while.

"Where were you stationed?" Lee asks.

"Malabang, Philippine Islands," my dad says.

"When?"

"Nineteen forty-five. We were preparing to invade Japan."

No one else speaks.

I stand next to my dad. The tourists, in polo shirts and light colored windbreakers, move in closer around us. Several hold digital cameras above their heads to take my father's picture. A man with a video recorder moves silently around Lee, who stands in front of us. He keeps his video recorder pointed on my dad.

"Were you a Navy pilot?" Lee asks.

"No, Marines," my dad's voice is still strong, clear.

"Marines!" Lee exclaims. His eyes open wide behind the lenses of his aviator glasses. He salutes my dad, "Semper Fi. So was I! What was your squadron?"

"VMSB244," my dad rattles each letter and number in a staccato. "We called ourselves the Bombing Banshees."

"Were you ever shot down?"

"Nope," Dad laughs. "But I did crash land, once."

"I never knew that," I whisper to my dad.

He nods at me, "You do now."

When I was eight months pregnant with my daughter, I wasn't allowed to fly.

"I'll take care of this," my dad said, clipping each word in that same staccato voice. He boarded a commuter jet for me and flew to North Carolina.

In a Charlotte medical clinic, he stood watch over the blood sample that was taken from the father of my child.

My daughter's father had disappeared when I refused to end the pregnancy. My father hired a lawyer, located him and flew to Charlotte to retrieve the blood sample that would prove paternity.

When I saw the twin vials of his red blood in the Styrofoam container my dad brought back, I cried. I remember looking up from the two long glass tubes at my dad, the Marine who never showed emotion. He was blinking his own wet eyes.

Dad waited outside the delivery room to hear if he had a granddaughter or a grandson. He brought her home from the hospital with me. Her grandfather took her on her first stroll in a baby carriage. He was there for her First Holy Communion and her graduation from high school. All events her father skipped.

"Did you know Pappy Boyington, the leader of the Black Sheep Squadron?" Lee asks my dad.

"Yes!" nods Dad with a smile. "I met him twice. He was my hero."

"Mine too! Here, folks, is the real deal. A World War II dive bomber pilot!"

"Ah," the crowd's voice echoes in the vast hangar. My dad releases his hold on the walker and stands tall, nodding as applause grows. I join in the clapping and he raises his hand for us to stop. He is beaming.

Essays

Clarinda Harriss: A Baltimore Treasure

J ust a day before meeting with Clarinda Harriss to discuss her literary career as one of Maryland's most eminent poets, the CityLit Project of Baltimore announced the First Annual Clarinda Harriss Poetry Prize and Chapbook Competition. I asked Ms. Harriss how this came about. Though she is 70 years old, she is one of the youngest 70 yr olds in history and she is not retiring from teaching or writing. She said that the contest was the idea of Gregg Wilhelm, the executive director of CityLit, and Dr. Michael Salcman, poet and board member. She felt honored to have the contest named for her. As she and her publishing company have done over the years, the contest is to give poets, of whatever age, to have a book of poetry published. The times are hard. Economics discourage literary publication of any type but certainly by unknown and aspiring poets. The contest hopes to rectify that, to give at least one worthy poet a moment in the sun. Clarinda's name gives the winner instant visibility and legitimacy.

Very active in both the "literary scene" and in academics, Clarinda is the author of 5 poetry collections and co-author of two academic books. She is also a member of the "Diva Squad," with her work forming a third of the second book of poems in the Diva Squad series conceived and edited by Dr. Chezia Thompson-Cager. Her teaching career spans 1960 to the present, and in 2009, she was one of two winners of the University System of Maryland's Regents' Award for Teaching. At Towson University she continues to mentor student poets and editors in the production of *Grub Street*, which is a consistent national award winning college literary magazine. In addition, she still volunteers, as she has for over 30 years, to assist prisoners in the Maryland penal system in writing and publishing their poetry and stories. She said that she " is now embarking on a project involving the women writers of the Maryland House of Correction for Women, having seen and been blown away by a play they recently wrote and starred in." She said also that she has "never been paid for any of my prison work, but it has been very extensive and very rewarding."

I asked Clarinda about her father, a noted Baltimore journalist who started his newspaper career as an assistant to H.L.Mencken. R.P.Harriss was the editor of the Duke University's literary magazine. This activity somehow attracted Mencken's attention and, like a baseball team signs a top pitching prospect, Mencken hired Clarinda's father straight from college. During the Depression her father was the editor of the Paris Herald, where he met Richard "Moko" Yardley, the legendary Baltimore newspaper cartoonist. Both of them came back to Baltimore and were fixtures at the Baltimore Sun. Mencken who resided in Baltimore introduced R.P. Harriss to Clarinda's mother, Margery, well-known as a Baltimore educator.

With all of this literary and newspaper talent in Clarinda's background it isn't difficult to see how writing became an integral part of her life. Clarinda said that at age 8 she was inspired to write a great verse epic in blank verse. Her mother told her it was free verse. Her grandmother said she should scale her ambitions back and write about kittens.

Initially her efforts were on a smaller scale. She went to Friends School on North Charles Street. Often the girls and boys of Friends school were bused to school sporting events and to the larger community's political events as Friends School took its religious and philosophic principles seriously. The students often endured a somewhat long bus ride. To relieve the tedium, though there was never a question of whether the tedium would be relieved—these were high-spirited kids now—, Clarinda wrote dirty lyrics that her friends would sing to familiar tunes.

Clarinda did her undergraduate studies at Goucher College. She received an M.A. at Johns Hopkins University in 1961. She started her career in teaching at Forest Park High School while attending Johns Hopkins. After graduation she continued at Forest Park. She loved teaching at that school. However, she had a transportation problem. She lived in northeast Baltimore; Forest Park is in extreme West Baltimore. Clarinda had a Morris Minor, A British made motor car that was designed for family use. Clarinda's car had seen many miles in its time and when she drove it, it was held together by rubber bands, bobby pins, and staples. Prayers were only partially successful in getting the car to its destination. As a consequence, Clarinda became acquainted with the Baltimore Transit Company. This didn't bode well for a long term career on the other side of town. She had small children and got a job more conveniently located at Towson High School. Then she taught at Goucher from 1967 to 70 as well as being what is termed even today a "Beltway Adjunct", a course here, a course there, tenure no where. That is how it is, starting out in an academic career.

Clarinda's father was a noted journalist and a writer of fiction. Her first publications were short stories. She still publishes 2 or 3 short stories a year, but she admits that she never felt comfortable with fiction. Her love of poetry was highly enhanced by Goucher English professor Sara DeFord, who was a medievalist and poet. In fact, Clarinda was one of the translator's of the Crofts' Classics' edition of "The Pearl". Poetry had advantages over fiction. Clarinda then, as now, had a busy life teaching, raising children. A young mother's life is not easy, though rewarding it may be. Poetry is, compared to fiction, short. In a small space of time she could write in the white heat of inspiration or coolly revise a poem. She says it is a "shorter take."

Michael Egan was a major mentor and influence. He ignited an already simmering passion for poetry. Egan founded the New Poets Series and was the first editor. Its purpose was to publish local Baltimore and Maryland poets. Before NPS there was little opportunity for a poet to bloom. Baltimore was for local writers a land of scant opportunity. Even Josephine Jacobsen, Baltimore's own and the first female poet laureate of the US, had to look to Louisiana State's university press to get her books published. Egan decided to change that. Clarinda said she started out doing much of the grunt work and fundraising for the Series; early financial backing which she secured included U.S. Laureate Josephine Jacobsen and famous humorist Ogden Nash. The first book was Michael Egan's "The Oldest Gesture". The proceeds from that book went to publish Clarinda's first solo effort "The Bone Tree". (That a press which she herself later headed published her first poetry collection remains a source of embarrassment, Clarinda says.) Clarinda took over as editor/director of NPS (now BrickHouse Books, Inc.) after Egan, for a variety of reasons, didn't have time for it. It was she who incorporated the press and secured its not-for-profit status, which made it eligible for NEA and local grants. Early in its corporate existence, such grants helped fund some of its publications and also its several series of readings and workshops, notably "Poetry at the Angel." We talked about the old Angel Bar itself. Henninger's Tavern now occupies the building. Clarinda mentioned how the two couples that owned the bar swapped spouses eventually. That wasn't a cause of its demise but it probably didn't make business run as smooth as it could have.

Clarinda and I talked about the Poetry at the Angel years, the mid-to-late 1970's. We reminisced about a number of the poets who participated in this three-year-long, every-Sunday series of readings at a bar in Fells Point. I asked if she was in contact with some of them. She gave updates on some. Dyane Fancey and she were the co-founders of the reading series. Josephine Jacobsen, Julia Randall, Devy Bendit, Andrei Codrescu, and Lucille Clifton, as well as performance poets including David Franks, were among the featured readers. Jan-Mitchell Sherrill , who is an associate dean at Point Park University in Pittsburgh now, had his first book of poems *Blind Leading The Blind* published by the New Poets Series in 1978. Since then he has had three other books brought out by Stonewall, *Friend of the Groom, Gunfire in Oz* and *The Kit Poems*. Stonewall is a subsidiary of Brickhouse Books, as are the New Poets Series and Chestnut Hills Press. Brickhouse Books is the umbrella corporation. Stonewall Books is dedicated to publishing poetry from a lesbian, gay or bisexual perspective. New Poets Series still has the mission of publishing a first book, but it is no longer restricted geographically to the Maryland area. The Chestnut Hills Press is an author-financed branch of BrickHouse but it isn't a vanity press; books it publishes are runners-up for a spot in the New Poets Series. Lynn Dowell was another poet from the Angel days. She is currently the Director of the Academic Advising Center at Towson University. She periodically teaches a Towson U. course on writing poetry. Clarinda lamented the death of Devy Bendit almost 25 years ago now. She said she had enormous talent and she seemed to be a very self-confident person, but she wasn't. She didn't survive one of her bouts of depression.

In the late 1980's Salmon, a press in Ireland, published Clarinda's *Night Parrot*. Michael Egan, whose own book *We Came Out Again To See The Stars* was published by Salmon, was instrumental in helping her getting her work published there. She said that she traveled to Ireland a couple of times with Egan and gave readings throughout the Republic. She said one of the most memorable was at the Clifden Poetry Festival where she shared billing on the multi-day program with Seamus Heaney, though she laughed and said his name was writ large, hers was writ small, but it was exciting. Clarinda then mentioned that last year Salmon published an anthology (*Salmon: A Journey In Poetry 1981-2007*) edited by Jessie Lendennie which included some of her poems and part of the unpublished book-length poem which Michael Egan was working on before he died, *Leviathan*.

We then talked about a new project with another Egan, Moira, Michael's daughter. Clarinda said that she and Moira are compiling and editing an anthology of erotic sonnets. They plan to include a couple of their own poems too. They will include historical examples from past centuries but they have also solicited and received numerous sonnets from contemporaries. Moira has a good network of contacts among Neo-Formalists. They are including such prominent writers as Marilyn Hacker and Kim Addonizio. They hope the prospective publisher will go along with their tentative title "Hot Sonnets."

Clarinda said she has fallen in love with the sonnet form. She calls her own sonnet series "69" because everything is based on a 6 or 9 syllable line. The sonnets are 15 line poems rather than the traditional 14. The volta, which is a turn or change of subject matter in an Italian or Petrarchan sonnet, occurs after line 6 or line 9. Her sonnets tend to be about interpersonal and family relationships; some are akin to flash fiction.

I asked her about her writing routine. Did she write every day? Same time every day? She said that there is no such regulated approach as her time hardly seems to be her own. She has teaching obligations and then a thousand and one other things. When she is in the white heat of writing she becomes as if possessed. She forgets to answer the phone or even think about anything else but the writing. Often though, during the school year, she does the same assignments that she prescribes to her classes. These include experiments in traditional or invented forms. One of the best places for doing a preliminary draft she has found is in an airplane. "Airplanes give a weird sense of privacy and perspective." One of Clarinda's children is a son who is an equine veterinarian. He and his wife lived in Argentina for awhile; now they live in New Zealand. Both destinations require a long flight. She has used and will use the long period of time in the air to write poems or fiction. Though the first draft is important, she loves revising. She is meticulous in assessing and altering the draft of a work.

Below are a few of her poems:

Talking Dirty

I wanted to write a talking-dirty sonnet,
most probably Petrarchan—dirty words
rhyme well, though dentally (a bit absurd—
they should be labial.) I'd get right on it
except that limericks have been there, done it,
and those hard sounds might cramp the sweet first third
of sex's poem, the slow swell, the blurred
divide between perhaps and have-to-have it.

And yet—what romance lacks a volta, vital
or fatal? Love's halves, asymmetrical
always, maintain a shaky poise; in time,
may teeter toward a murderous punch-line.
The poem writes itself. We lie in trance,
but love, fuck, trouble hum their assonance.

Reader Writer Traveler Thief

Puberty gave a boost to her kleptomania. No more
messing with glass gems & candy cigarettes: the real
things, plus dirty paperbacks from the drugstore.
Just for the fun of it. Always gave the swag away.

Fast forward thirty years. Discretion, caution, even
perhaps a mite of conscience—she really meant
to return the tattered classic she borrowed from
a tiny library in New Zealand, where she stole

summer from January. What to bring her lover
as a souvenir? Careful, no mementos for his wife!
In the duty-free at the last stop before home
she jettisoned Middlemarch, along with notes for
some fatuous ekphrastics on Maori art, and sleight—
handed a box of chocolates into her overnight.

2600 Block, October 6, 2008

In the block where I'd lived, a baby's born
and killed. He's found in a garbage can behind
St. John's, whose brick and iron cloister winds
to the alley. Its privacy was utter, and well known.
My parents and I, beyond the table where we dined,
could see Old (Homeless) George, who drank and mourned
for F. D. R. When beaten, robbed, he warned
us Place ain't safe. And this was forty-nine.
I grew to be a smart-ass kid who used
to hide and seek and smoke in St. John's dark,
the one girl in a pack of boys. For a lark
they tore off my shirt to check (they said) "the view."
Soon we moved away. My P's complained of noise.
And I re-learned to like the salty smell of boys.

Darryl? Darryl?

Sixteen, you were a black flamingo kid
in puffy Elizabethan shorts you'd Scarlet O-
Hara'd out of your mother's drapes. Wow—
the audience of tenth graders was awed:
Hushed, till at the end, they stood and roared.
So gaudy, so improbable, you vowed
to knock us all dead with Shakespeare. Now,
the first and only Lear I recognize (yes! felled
by stroke!; then, all of Shakespeare's Henrys.
Such lush soliloquies! such gorgeous rages!
That black velvet voice!
Your phonecall's
whispered message—Write me a poem—frenzied
me. An exit line? There is no answer when I call
you back. What a killer way to leave the stage.

69: Night Blindness

I've turned old enough to share the dusk
with my father and his cataracts.
Our hazel eyes squint, turn milky green.
Night driving in the rain is terror,
two dimensions of lethal shimmer.
Indoors, doors silhouette looming shapes.

Woods are full of wolves where
once lightning bugs were all
that was needed to read
the lips of a lover.
My father told about
raccoon hunting at ten:
old Chet's aim was perfect,
so the boy thought all black
men could see in the dark.

69: Feet

There's something about the way your feet
  hug my ears that makes me feel oddly
    safe. They stop out all bad things.
      I'm a sort of child, staring up
        under the canopy, which
          might cover a wagon
            or a queen who
              never said
                "Let
              them eat cake."
            No one could drop
          dead in such a position,
        there's a limit to how silly
      the dead are allowed to be, & yet
    the yellow smell of each other's soles
  reminds us of the thirteen steps to where
we will be crowned by willow wands and slain.

Book Reviews

Stranger At Home, An Anthology: American Poetry With An Accent, edited by Gritsman, Weingarten, Brown, Firan. Interpoezia Inc. and Numina Press, New York 2008, $15.95.

The anthology presents English poems by poets for whom English is a second language, though the poets in this book are, for the most part, as fluent in English as any native born speaker. The most recognizable names are Nina Cassian, Andrei Codrescu, Anselm Hollo, and, for Maryland readers, Danuta E. Kosk-Kosicka. The range of poetry is from the superbly written traditional pantoum "Stillbirth" by Laure-Anne Bosselaar to poetry that leaps with irrationality like the phrases of Codrescu.

A main editorial concern was to present immigrant voices that show both a mastery and a metamorphosis of the English language. Though Andrey Gritsman asserts in his introduction that poems can not be translated from one language to another, the non-native poets retain much of their previous sensibility and adopt the new culture, its concerns, expressions, producing an accented voice that is as rich tasting as an ethnic dish. Of course poetry is not a trivial foodstuff but the pulse of being human made vocal. The poets in this anthology run the gamut from being as American as any native born writer to being the voice of the immigrant trying to fit into the new society. Wang Ping in a poem titled "On A Playground in Park Slope, Brooklyn, A Retired Neurologist From Beijing Is Cursing" starts off like this:

> Sit still, you little pumpkin shit face.
> Stop fidgeting. And stop
> Whining about your sore feet.
> If your mother hadn't left you outside
> A shoe factory, dumping you like bad luck,
> You'd be digging mud and collecting cow dung
> In some godforsaken place.

And after many very vivid lines contrasting the life the little girl would have had in China with the life as an adopted child, the poem ends with these lines:

> So Lili, my silly pumpkin face,
> Wipe your nose and walk.
> Time to practice again.
> You're stubborn, and proud. Good!
> Don't ever let your parents' frown seal your lips.
> Don't let their butter and steak mush your brain.

You're Chinese, a Chinese peasant girl.
Now take your steps.
It's all right to stumble, to fall.
Here's my hand.
Take it.

I'm your countrywoman.
I am your Mother.

The poets come from Asia, Russia, Eastern and Central Europe, South America. There are poems with the heaviness of Holocaust memories on their hearts. There is a poem that gives a unique treatment to the 9-11 tragedy. There is a poem titled "Photograph Of Myself, Age Four, Asleep In My Father's Arms". There is the poem "Florida" by Adrian Sangeorzan which sums up one type of immigrant experience.

When we grow old
We'll retire to Florida.
At first we'll send our spirits there
On short holidays
In search of youth without aging
And life without death.

We are a generation with strong and white bones
We invented hurricanes, globalization and saltwater
That we will pass on
To our children or to some foundation
Which will love us with moderation.
The hot sand and the sun will remind us of
The 60's, feminism and the sexual revolution
When the spoiled hormones of communism
Swarmed under our skin giving us true sensations
Which our mothers unaware
Greased up with butter
On our bread.

Today everything in America is big
The towers, the beaches, people's bellies
The toilet seats
The ideas working on steroids
Only the spirits still play in the sand
With golden pickaxes.

This is the place for the great retreat
The last survivors
Cured of all of life's melanoma
Quietly play bridge at the edge of the world
Their nephews listen to hip-hop on iPods.
We are all so digitalized.
Seagulls blinded by cataract perch
On Poseidon's back
Whose only remains are a floating shoulder blade
And the name of a casino.

We are the next elephants
We'll slowly migrate to Miami
Through the slippery funnel of America.
We still make love without Viagra
Right on the coils of the old watches
Which we'll wind up
They'll continue to tick under our king-size beds
Like a Chinese perpetual mobile.

On the beach the sand
Escaped from hourglasses
Will build solid castles
Where all the world's languages will be spoken
From which we'll choose for our ears
Some gorgeous coral idioms.

During our last years
We will tan well all over
We will cremate ourselves unnoticeably
More beautiful than Tutankhamen.

The book is 152 pages of poetry and occasional commentary by some of the authors on what they feel their relationship is to language. Alexei Tsvetkov writes "Learning the art of poetry in a nonnative language is... akin to learning an entirely new kind of art, not unlike trying to become a musician after a lifetime of painting, and much of similarity is deceptive." However, the poets in this anthology make it look easy because there is quality poetry here.

There is another aspect to this book, which makes it even more valuable to read, and that is the presentation of so many different styles and approaches to poetry. Some of the poets have been grounded in Russian absurdism and like movements. Here are a few stanzas from Eugene Ostashevsky's "Ballad"

SHE SAID:

I was attached to a rock like a limpet
Around me ran waters limpid

I could not move not even limping
I became Eleatic and Olympic

I could not C
I could not D
I could not E
I could not F

I saw a knight
Of special K
He wore a scuba
He was OK

I took his scuba
His face turned blue
I cried, Where are you
Scooby-Doo?

The above is not the traditional poetry of English 101 but it is verbal play and smacks of contemporary sensibility.

The anthology presents diverse styles, voices, influences. Any reader who loves poetry will find treasure in this book. Perhaps a poem or two will open new doors of appreciation. Just as these poets came as immigrants to a new country and language, so too should readers come and experience and adapt themselves to these new poetic visions. Human experience is not static.

Lidia Kosk, *Słodka woda, słona woda / Sweet Water, Salt Water*, translated and edited by Danuta E. Kosk-Kosicka, with three short stories translated by Wojciech Winiewski, Jan Winiewski, and Piotr Kosicki, respectively.

The most remarkable attribute of Lidia Kosk's new book of poetry *Słodka woda, słona woda / Sweet Water, Salt Water* is the beauty of the poetry. True Beauty is so rare in modern or contemporary writing. This book is not pretty poetry, not a Sunday painter's poetry. It is not really impressionist in the Monet sense. We aren't talking about dabs of imagery and the haze of an aesthetic sensibility. Lidia Kosk's work has an elemental beauty that is more akin to nature and inspiration than learned artifice. Now that is not to say that she isn't an accomplished poet, because she is, but to emphasize that her poetry grows out of her heart, not imposed by detached intellect. She is a poet from a country not self-indulgent and pseudo-sophisticated. Her country, Poland, her generation, experienced World War II, Nazi occupation and then the dull grey tyranny of the Communists. Negative emotions like grief color her vision but everything in her poetry points the way out of any such suffocation. Part of her endurance may be due to religious faith, as expressed in the poem Of the *City's Spirit*, and part may be due to the closeness, to the love, literally, for her native soil, but much has to do with what is in her heart. Her heart can only express itself through and as beauty for that is what it is, a natural beauty, a bloom of human nature.

The book is bi-lingual. Ms. Kosk's daughter Danuta Kosk-Kosicka, a poet herself, translated the Polish poetry into English. The translation is more than competent; it is first rate poetry. Only one word in the whole book is just a little out of kilter with American English. In line 3 of the second poem the word "Fido's" seems odd. Presumably it is a dog's impassioned barking that is meant. I point this out only because every other word, phrase, poem is inspired and the translation carries the imagination of the Polish poet into American English as if the poem's native language was English. The prose on the jacket front flap and inside the book was translated by Danuta E. Kosk-Kosicka, who also edited the book. The three short stories in Chapter IV were translated by three other individuals. Special mention should be made of Wojciech Wisniewski who translated the prose of *Lily*, while Ms. Kosk-Kosicka rendered the poetry in that piece into English. The book is published by ASTRA of Łódź, Poland.

There are really 3 components of the book, the English being one. There is a wealth of photography accompanying the poems and on the front and back covers. Most of the photos were taken by Lidia Kosk herself. The cover is of a sunset and ripples of gentle waves lacing the

Baltic Sea shore. The back cover is of Ms Kosk by a river in the Polish countryside. Throughout the book there are other photos of tree trunks and footprints on the sand of beach. These are interesting images, but the memorable images are in the poems. The third component is the original Polish on the left hand pages facing the translation on the right.

The book is divided into four sections. The first is called **Birth of the World**. The poems in this section are filled with a pristine beauty almost unconscious of history. The first poem is titled "Paradise." The human is present immediately.

Into clear water
of each other's irises
they dive
the overflow distills
in the morning dew

Celestial blue
strokes the heads
of forget-me-nots
snow remnants blush
into apple blooms
the sun of summer
does not burn
the earth they stroll
the rains of autumn spare
the fruit
so they can reach for it

It is a remarkable lyric. I see of at least two ways of interpreting it. The first is the Adam and Eve scenario with the ironic mention of "The fruit". The second is of two lovers, and the fruit then becomes not a disguised threat but a wondrous sharing. Beyond interpretation is the gorgeous imagery. Paraphrasing any of it, because it is very understandable and elemental, is like analyzing comedy in that the beauty would be bleached out of the poetry. The imagery is not intellectual. Order and precision are admirable qualities but what we have here is the bloom of a garden, not the decoration of a house.

Poem after poem in this section has this wondrous vision. Some poems occur in winter and the Fall from grace and childhood and pure romantic love is intimated but the poems affirm the miracle of it all. The beauty is tangible, not some ascetic distillation. The poem below illustrates this:

Out of the Dream Dusk

Dusk falls in the stillness of forest
around the cluster of trees and brush
and settles my thoughts

Feelings stream in
from faraway times
reveal in retiring light
shadows of cows
in the meadows of remembrance

The closeness permeates:
fur odor after a hot day
chains rattling
a human connection

Strokes of the church clock
from a faraway tower
organize time

The sensations of the present evoke the past. It is, in a sense, a very Proustian passage, though the world recalled is Old World Poland and the memories of childhood there. Is it significant that the clock is a "church clock?" Perhaps the passage of time, or the consciousness of it, expels humanity from that Paradise that began the book.

A very seemingly simple poem, *I Bent to Pick Up a Lump Of Earth*, closes this first section. This poem is so simple in conception but it is a haunting poem, one with great meaning. That clump of earth symbolizes her childhood and everything that she has learned and that she is. She "yearned for its company/on the long road."

Section 2 **From The Cradle of Earth** contains the imperfect world that is the reality that dreams cannot shake. However, this section is not about grief and loss so much as the battle between such negative emotions and the ever present joy still available and sometimes found by the heart. The title poem explains the theme of this section succinctly.

From the Cradle of Earth

From the Cradle of Earth
pupils follow the light of stars
on the open umbrella of outer space
beneath

the clouds mature
glow crimson with pain
from the birth of beauty and dread
the imminence of passing away

sand sifting from the hourglass
rocks the cradle of earth

Section 3 is called **Only the Memory Takes Note**. History, both personal and national, permeates the poetry here. In *Gloria Victis* the Warsaw Uprising of 1944 is shown to be the harbinger of August 1994, when Poland is truly free. Some of the history of Poland may be unfamiliar to American readers but the particulars won't mar an appreciation of the poetry. The internet is always available to look up a strange name or an unknown event; however, the poetry may be set in history, but the poetry reverberates in the heart, in the soul. This section is both elegy and affirmation. Though Polish history has had bleak moments in Lidia Kosk's lifetime, and though she acknowledges the sorrows, she is anything but a defeated spirit. The poems are so interwoven with the ascendency of first one emotion and then another, but a beauty and a strength prevail in her heart. Evil and pain are not glossed over but the poet transcends them, like a flower after a grueling winter. The poem below illustrates this:

Embalmed in Fog

you float in through the window
open on this March night
our thoughts interweave
rejoin our journey halted
by the stillness of the Styx

your arms
shield me
from the stiffening chill
stop the icicles from wounding
my heart

Section 4 is titled **From the Storyteller's Volume**. It contains both prose and poetry. History and the lyric are transformed into folklore. Narrative and symbolism are the keys here. The story Lily is as beautiful as any of the poems in the book. It is on one level similar to a child's tale but it is very much the story of a mature poet.

I've just given a short sketch of the book. There is much to explore, much to marvel at. Paraphrasing the title of the book, and borrowing from William Blake, I would call these poems songs of innocence and songs of experience.

C.E. Chaffin, *Unexpected Light: Selected Poems and Love Poems 1998–2008*, Diminuendo Press, 2009, ISBN 978-0-9821352-7-3, 138 pages, paperback $12.00.

R etired psychiatrist, one-time editor of a leading webzine, self-confessed bipolar mental patient, admirer of T.S. Eliot and Pablo Neruda, C.E. Chaffin (full name Craig Erick Chaffin—first monickers he says he detests!), is a cool cat and a fine poet. Although we have yet to meet in the flesh, I have known C.E. through cyberspace and been in occasional correspondence with him since I joined the Internet poetry scene in the 1990's. Not so long ago I even promised to have an active discussion with him on one of his favorite works of literature, Eliot's "Four Quartets"— but as other projects beckoned, it was one more vow broken! It was some ten years ago that I discovered Melic Review, a fine on-line magazine and poetry workshop that unfortunately was sabotaged when it was attacked by spammers. I also must fess up that among my poetic credits (and a parallel I share with Dr. Chaffin) is a parody of Eliot's "The Waste Land" that can be found among the Melic archives. Chaffin kindly, and I believe wisely, continues to maintain the old archives—there's some fine work there, including examples of his own poetry.

C.E. and his wife Kathleen Lenore, also a poet, lived for a number of years in Mexico but after their children grew up and left the nest, they relocated to the Redwoods region of Northern California. They also had the sad misfortune to lose a daughter a couple of years ago. This book is dedicated "in Memory of Rachel Chaffin, 1977–2007." There are also a couple of poems, painful to read, in which the poet wrestles with the death of his daughter. Check out this lean and memorable piece:

On Rachel's Death

The hole
in the ground
left by the tree

the hole left
by her life
or my life
or any life

always lacks
dirt enough
to cover
the uprooted

root-crown
again.

Loss is a coin
tossed down
a depthless well

you listen
for a splash
that
never

comes.

Many poets choose to write in a linear format, but their "skinny po-ems" are often merely a stylistic choice and not integral to the meaning or impact of the written work. But here in this poem, this stark, bereaved father's poem, every painful word counts. The linear pattern works ex-tremely effectively to record the poet and father's feelings of loss. This isn't manufactured emotion. It is real. It is tangible. And difficult to read for that reason.

Chaffin mostly writes using a longer line, perhaps reflecting the works of his poetic heroes, Eliot and Neruda. Also being of the generation he is, there are war-related poems, notably the following poem about Washington, D.C.'s iconic black wall Vietnam War Memorial. The poet himself, in the text of the poem, admits the piece is somewhat polemical.

But so what... he is writing from the heart, damn it!

At the Vietnam War Memorial

Black granite stretches its harsh, tapering wings
up to pedestrian-level grass
but sucks me down, here, at the intersection of names.
I forgive, I must, though I wish something
could heal this wound in the earth.

Behold, all theorists, the price of theory:
extreme unction by napalm and blood,
vets shipped home whole or in pieces.
The VA grants prostheses
but not minds free of horror.

In jungles tumescent, through villages

of straw, by the Mekong where catfish
sleep in mud-heaven, we tramped,
disarming mines and flushing tunnels,
killing women and children
for potential collaboration,
smoking Thai-stick until stuporous—
still, the sound of Charlie
played on every frond.

Beat against this polished rock, America,
this vast projective surface for your sins,
wear your bloody heart out.
It's not how many died
but that they died in vain, achieving
nothing except our grief for them.

It's said you cannot write a good poem
until recollected in tranquility.
Let this then be a bad poem, bad as the war,
dividing author from reader and reader from page.
Let it drive a wedge between fathers and sons.
Let fathers mistake rebellion for disloyalty,
let sons mistake honor for stupidity,
let senators mistake appropriation for commitment,
let mothers confuse waste with sacrifice,
let sisters turn to prostitution to forget.

Let teachers suicide in public in partial recompense,
let preachers castrate themselves for passive assent,
let everything in America that breathes
hang its head in irrefragable shame.
Here is the legacy of your assumptions,
here the necropolis of your dark-suited wisdom:
A city set in a pit cannot be hid.

Notice how, metaphorically, the monument is a "wound in the earth" just as the daughter's death was the gouging out of a tree trunk. Chaffin draws on the influence of of Eliot well here (April is after all "the cruelest month"), expertly using the natural world to reflect human pain.

Unexpected Light is both a book of love poems and a book about the poet wrestling with his own demons. Few of the poems included in the book are much more forceful and memorable than the following two works, both of which draw on the poet's feelings of fear and paranoia—

Eternal Recurrence

Psychologists call mania
a defense against depression
but I find that silly.
There is no defense
against depression
and no adequate metaphor
for its recurrence, but I'll try:

You love someone with all your heart.
They are brutally murdered.
After an interminable grief
they magically reappear
and you fall down on your knees
and thank God with tears.

The second time is worse.

After the third funeral
you dread their resurrection
as much as their death
and love becomes a poisonous thing.
You would drive a stake
through their heart
if only you could.

Baby

It's 4:30 AM, pitch-black and cold.
I spoon against your body
wishing there were no cotton
to separate us, not even skin.

I want to crawl up your tunnel
and hide deep in your belly
before the sun exposes me.
Let me re-gestate, please.

Maybe this time it will be better,
maybe this time I won't end up

clinging to you like a life raft
in the shipwrecked night,
forty and terrified.

If you should wake
and want to make love
I may stay inside forever.

It's not all seriousness in the world of C. E. Chaffin. There's a wry sense of humor in among the pain and the tragedy. Consider one more poem, "Tonic" reflecting the poet's trauma as well as joy. It's been a long, hard road—

Tonic

I will love myself today.
Here are some fuzzy slippers
and a lollipop,
a warm hug and a wet kiss.
Let me tuck this
old familiar blanket
around my shoulders
and read this poem
before I nap.

Whatever I do today,
I'll approve.
If I spill milk, I'll clap.
If I button my shirt wrong
it's a new style.
If I wet my pants
it was on purpose.

My, how well I walk!
How well I speak!
It's so good to be
good to myself.
Where have I been
all these sad, long years?

These poems and numerous other examples in *Unexpected Light* confirm the stature of C.E. Chaffin's work.

If I had a reservation about C.E. Chaffin's *Unexpected Light*, it would be this: although the collection is jam packed with fine poetry, the typeface is a bit on the small size and could have done with being a notch or two larger than it is. Still that's a relatively minor gripe about a major collection.

Laurie Byro, *The Bird Artists*, LaurieByro.com, $10.00 plus $3.00 shipping & handling.

This is a slim book but like the diminutive Laurie Byro herself, it is packed with power. The title poem well exemplifies what Ms. Byro brings to the table as a poet, a vibrant personal perception of the world enlightened by age-old myth and needle-point observation of animal and bird imagery:

The Bird Artists

When my skin no longer fits, I carry a bag of bones,
to the edge of the ocean. I steal the breath from a gull.
On the beach a mother bends to help a young boy
bundle up a baby cormorant. I watch as they cradle it,

hold a wing into the air and fling it eastward.
I thought you could teach me how to fly. I made you
out of sand dunes and red clay. My husband sleeps.
I conjure up you, Merwin, and you, Merlin.

Palm trees and ancient words, a black cauldron
of seawater and fire. You spread the fan of the cormorant's
wing and arrange your pigments and brushes, stroke

each feather with woodland brown or green.
I feel my skin begin to loosen. I pick away the lice,
curl back the sclerotic welt of paint.

For the "Bird Artists", the poet was honored by first place in the March 2007 InterBoard Poetry Competition (IBPC). In her remarks about the poem, judge Pascale Petit, the French/Welsh poet who lives in the UK, said in part: "Every line is weighted with a surprising image or action. Even though the effect is mythic, there's a precise highly wrought feel to this poem. Not a word or space is wasted. Vulnerable, visceral and ethereal, it lingers in the imagination and draws me back to marvel at its compact power."

Now here I have to admit some personal bias toward Laurie and her poetry. On a speaking trip several years ago, I made a special stop in Hoboken, New Jersey, to meet Laurie and her husband, Mike, and we were photographed by Mike by the Hudson River. On that occasion, Laurie wore a headdress of feathers, appropriate for a poet who deals so rawly and beautifully with tales of the bird and animal kingdom.

In the following poem, Ms. Byro adapts the story in Charlotte Brontë's Jane Eyre to make her own piece of memorable literature:

Jane Eyre's Daughter

I kept thinking I was Jane Eyre's daughter.
I suspected my mother really wanted a son.

Fascinated with attics I foraged through chests
with breakable locks filled with baptism gowns,

sniffed among moth-balls for matchboxes
from exotic pool halls, hints of adoption papers.

I kept thinking I was Jane Eyre's daughter, trying
to find myself in the travel section of the library

searching for a honeymoon in Katmandu.
St John bristled when I wanted our first dance

to be to the tune of Sexual Healing. Every one
broke off the engagement before the tickets'

non-refundable fee kicked in. I kept thinking
I was Jane Eyre's daughter. Weddings

were unpleasant since I would rush in late,
panting "I object" for the sheer joy of seeing

horrified expressions, maids tearfully ringing
hands and not bells. Today as I left another

thwarted nuptial, four fine blackbirds watched me
from the wires which connected my rubber ball

heart to my deeply anticipated "his". My mother,
Aunt Reed, dear crazy Bertha, and daddy

in his mourning coat: the grim four posed perfectly
still like chessmen while I crossed my bosom

which throbbed like the July sun and waited
with little patience for mother to play her next card.

And here we'll look at one more poem that illustrates Ms. Byro's adept use of animal and nature imagery and the mesmerising way she interweaves myth and reality to create something fresh and memorable:

Wolf Dreams

I wasn't sure what he wanted of me; the ice
in winter birches had made the forest slouch
into spring. All that winter I peeled

and sucked papery bark for the sweet taste.
I recognized him from his red tongue,
the furtive runs when I entered his dream

and we crawled along the forest floor, repenting
the dark. I had nothing to bargain with,
no deal to make him human. The night

was filled with briars and salt. In the summer
the air became thick with honeysuckle, slick
with mating. Beetles droned in messy beds

of clover. We slunk along, weeds stroking
my belly. I hadn't yet decided which life
was better. Grass combed the plume of my tail.

The nights were crystal sharp. I waggled
my slit high, what was left of my breasts pushed
into a pile of decaying leaves. Who cared

how many and how often, I was not entirely his.
Eyes of owls glittered in the sleep of trees, tree frogs
sang in a green-robed choir. The moon clamped

its yellow tooth into my shoulder. I took the whole
night inside. What was to become of us? I had
packed away my white Juliet cap and veil for just

such an occasion. I held him like a warm
peach in my palm, longed for his juice to run
down my chin. Most nights I didn't care about

the names they gave me. I held my fingers
out to him, felt the tug as my ring fell off, carried
my limbs down to the entrance of his den,

planted a birch just outside his home
as a token of my loyalty. I was free
of the chains of consequence. I gave birth

to his amber-eyed bastard who without hesitation
he devoured. When he becomes old and says
he always dreams of me, I shall make myself

a meal of him, savor his voluptuous tongue,
and suck all the bitterness from his bones.
He will not make such promises again.

Laurie Byro's voice is a unique one. It's no wonder that she consistently garners recognition in the monthly IBPC awards. She deserves even greater attention in the poetry world at large. May it come about.

Contributor Notes

William L. Alton has been writing now for nearly twenty-five years, recently publishing work in *The Poet's Canvas, Red River Review, The Oklahoma Review, Whalelane* and *Amarillo Bay*. Currently, he lives in Forest Grove, Oregon with his wife and three sons.

James Bell returned to poetry after a twenty year hiatus and has been making up for lost time in the last dozen years. He was born in Scotland, and has lived in Devon, England for many years. A chapbook, *the just vanished place*, appeared in 2008 and will be followed by a forthcoming full collection in 2010 entitled *fishing for beginners*.

Sara Bernert is a college student at Seattle University, studying theatre and creative writing.

Danny Birchall lives and works in London. His work has been published in *Nineties Poetry, Mechanics Institute Review, nthposition* and *Right Hand Pointing*, and performed at various venues in London.

Jenn Blair is from Yakima, WA. She is currently a Park Hall Fellow at the University of Georgia where she teaches British Literature. She has published in *The Tusculum Review, Copper Nickel, SNR Review, The Fairfield Review, Miranda*, and *MELUS* among others.

Bob Bradshaw is a programmer living in Redwood City, CA. He is a big fan of both the Rolling Stones and afternoon naps. Mick may not be gathering moss, but Bob is. Recent work of his can be found at *Eclectica, Slow Trains, Subtle Tea, Orange Room Review* and *into the teeth of the wind*.

Lisa Marie Brodsky received her MFA in Poetry from the University of Wisconsin-Madison. Her poetry has been published in *The North American Review, Illya's Honey, The Southern Ocean Review, Circle Magazine, Born Magazine*, among others. Her chapbook, "We Nod Our Dark Heads," was published by Parallel Press in 2008 and her full-length collection, "Motherlung," is forthcoming from Salmon Publishing in 2012.

Janet Butler, after spending many years in central Italy, where she developed a passion for watercolors and poetry, relocated to the Bay Area, California. She currently teaches TESL and Italian in San Francisco, balancing her passion for watercolors and poetry with walks with Fulmi, a beautiful abandoned Springer Spaniel/English Setter mix she brought back with her from Italy. Among recent publications are *Literary Mary, Sage Trail, Rattlesnake Review, ken*again*, and *Poets Ink*. Future publications include *The 13th Warrior, Plainsongs*, and *Yellow Mama*. "Eden Fables" was published as an online chapbook by Language & Culture, 2007, *Collection: Ekphrastic Poems* by Robert Schuler and Janet Butler was published (by invitation of the editor) by Canvas Press Collection Series, 2007, and "Shadowline" by Gatto Publishing, Scotland (2007) as an eBook.

Clay Carpenter is a newspaper copy editor in Corpus Christi, Texas. His poems have appeared in literary magazines including *Facets, Apple Valley Review, Falling Star* and *decomP*.

C.E. Chaffin, born in Ventura, California, in 1954, turned 54 in October 2008 and has white in his beard to prove it. He graduated from UCLA in 1976, Summa Cum Laudanum, Fine-Bit-of-Krappa, winning the top honors award in English, "The Edward Niles Hooker Award," though he was not in the honors program. He received other awards in medical school, in psychiatric residency, and later as a medical director. He taught Family Medicine at UCI and was named a Fellow of the American Academy of Family Physicians before the age of 40. Due to chronic spinal pain and manic-depression, he elected to retire on disability from medicine in his early 40s, which led to his discovery of the literary internet. Chaffin published and edited the webzine *Melic Review* for eight years until its recent extended hiatus, a journal that has distinguished itself not only by its content but through the work of participating poets at its board in winning and/or placing in the monthly InterBoard Poetry Competition (IBPC) repeatedly. He has won one poetry contest (*Desert Moon Review*, 2002) and was nominated for a Pushcart Prize by *Rose and Thorn*. He quit counting publications several years ago but has been featured poet in journals over twenty times.

Tobi Cogswell is a Pushcart nominee and co-recipient of the first annual Lois and Marine Robert Warden Poetry Award from Bellowing Ark. Her work can be read in *SPOT Lit(erary) Mag(azine), Penumbra, Spoon River Poetry Review* and *Sugar House Review* among others, and is upcoming in *Illyas Honey, Ozone Park, Rhino, Slab, Blue Earth Review* and *Off the Coast*. She has three chapbooks and her full-length poetry collection *"Poste Restante"* is available from Bellowing Ark Press. She is the co-editor of San Pedro River Review.

John J. Conley is the Francis J. Knott Professor of Philosophy at Loyola University in Maryland. His recent philosophical monographs include *Adoration and Annihilation* (University of Notre Dame Press, 2009) and *The Suspicion of Virtue* (Cornell University Press, 2002). Recently produced plays include *Final Arrangements* (Run-of-the-Mill Theater, Baltimore, 2009), *Arthritic* (Vestige Group Theater, Austin, 2008), and *O'Boylan's Finest* (Heartland Theater, Bloomington, 2007). He has published poetry in French and English in many journals, including *Windfall, Jewelweed*, and *Ampersand*.

Elizabeth Costello is a short story writer living in Dublin, Ireland. Her work has appeared in the Irish literary journal *Southword* and has been broadcast on Irish national radio. She has also been shortlisted for the Sean O'Faolain International Short Story Competition 2008.

Caryn Coyle's essay, "Forty-Five Years Ago" was published the Summer, 2008 issue of *Loch Raven Review*. She has also been published in *The Santa Fe Writers Program Literary Journal, JMWW, Preface, Damozel, Smile Hon,You're in Balti-*

more and her work is forthcoming in *Midway Journal* and *Gargoyle*. She won the 2009 Maryland Writers Association Short Fiction Contest.

Dan Cuddy has had poems published in the *Loch Raven Review, Manorborn*, and in numerous other publications. He reads two of his poems on the CD anthology *Words On War* produced by BirdHouse Studios. He is the author of a book of poems, *Handprint On The Window*, 2003.

Holly Day is a travel writing instructor living in Minneapolis, Minnesota, with her husband and two children. Her newest book is *Walking Twin Cities*.

Jim Doss is co-editor of *Loch Raven Review*. His work has appeared in *Poetry East, Words-Myth, Poems Niedergasse*, and other publications. He earns his living as a software engineer, and lives with his wife and three children in Maryland.

Dawn Dupler's works have appeared in *Loch Raven Review, The Writeside Up Magazine, Static Movement, Diddledog, The Flask Review, Glassfire's Print Anthology, Long Story Short, T-Zero, The Aggregated Press*. She currently studies classical music, voice, and photography while enjoying other forms of expression.

Walter Durk was born in New York City and has since lived in Asia and a few areas of the United States. He is a graduate of the University of Missouri and lives in the Atlanta area.

David Eberhardt works at the Baltimore City Jail in the Inmate Programs Dept., ex-con—21 months in federal prison for pouring blood on draft files, pardoned by Pres. Reagan in '83 (did Reagan ask him for a pardon?); collects books, plays the piano, is on the left (left where?) (where is he going?).

Nina Forsythe has an MFA from Bennington and her poems have appeared in a variety of literary magazines, including *Taproot, Chiron Review, 5AM, Puerto del Sol*, and most recently *Broken Bridge Review*. Her poem "Wedding" was recently nominated for a Pushcart Prize. She has also published translations in *The Nicaraguan Academic Journal* and a review in *Review Revue*. While these poems came out of her experience of living in Nicaragua for three years, she currently lives in Frostburg, MD, where she's working on a chapbook.

Liz Gallagher is from Ireland but now lives in the Canary Islands, Spain. She has poetry, fiction and non-fiction work published or forthcoming in *The Stinging Fly* (Featured Poet Winter 08/09), *Magma, Stirring, Nöo, The Mad Hatter's Review, The Pedestal Magazine, Nth Position, The SHOp*, and *The Oxfam Calendar 2009* and others. She was selected for the *Best New Poets 2007 Anthology* (Meridian Press, Virginia University). Her first full collection, titled *The Wrong Miracle*, will be published by Salt Publishing this year.

Kavita Gandhi is a MD/PhD student at the University of Maryland in Baltimore, currently performing scientific research in the area of malaria vaccines, and has written poetry from a very young age.

Christopher T. George is co-editor of *Loch Raven Review*. George was born in Liverpool, England in 1948 and now lives in Baltimore, Maryland, near Johns Hopkins University, with his wife Donna and two cats. Chris works full-time as a medical editor in Washington, DC. He has been writing and publishing poetry since he attended Loyola College, Baltimore, and studied with Sister Maura Eichner at the College of Notre Dame, as well as with poets Elliot Coleman and Marion Buchman. His poems have appeared in numerous publications in the United States and Great Britain. He is also a published historian and a lyricist for a new musical, *Jack-The Musical*, about Jack the Ripper. George also is the Editor of Desert Moon Review writer's workshop.

Howie Good, a journalism professor at the State University of New York at New Paltz, is the author of seven poetry chapbooks, including *Tomorrowland* (2008) from Achilles Chapbooks in print and *The Torturer's Horse* (2009) from Recycled Karma Press online.

Tracey Gratch lives in Quincy, MA with her husband and their four young children. Her poems have appeared or are forthcoming in *Lucid Rhythms, Snakeskin, The Poetry Porch: Sonnet Scroll, Pirene's Fountain, Boston Literary Magazine*, and *Annals of Internal Medicine*.

John Grochalski's poems have appeared in *Avenue, The Smoking Poet, Thieves Jargon, The Lilliput Review, The New Yinzer, The Blue Collar Review, The Deep Cleveland Junkmail Oracle, The ARTvoice, Modern Drunkard Magazine, The American Dissident, Words-Myth, My Favorite Bullet, The Main Street Rag, Underground Voices, Eclectica, Zygote In My Coffee, the Kennesaw Review, Octopus Beak Inc., Re)Verb, Clockwise Cat, Ink Sweat and Tears, Cherry Bleeds, Indite Circle, Lit Up, One Night Stanzas, American Tanka, Tattoo Highway, Lit Up, Ghoti, Why Vandalism, The Delinquent*, and the *Orange Room Review*. His short fiction has appeared in the *Pittsburgh Post-Gazette, Fictionville, Bartleby Snopes, Retort, The Battered Suitcase, The Big Stupid Review, Pequin*, and will be forthcoming in the anthology *Living Room Handjob*. His column The "Lost Yinzer" appears quarterly in *The New Yinzer*. His book of poems *The Noose Doesn't Get Any Looser After You Punch Out* is out via Six Gallery Press and his chapbook *Meditations On Misery With Women* is due from Tainted Coffee Press in the summer of 2010.

Christine Hamm is a PhD candidate in English Literature at Drew University. She won the MiPoesias First Annual Chapbook Competition with her manuscript, *Children Having Trouble with Meat*. Her poetry has been published in *The Adirondack Review, Pebble Lake Review, Lodestar Quarterly, Poetry Midwest, Rattle*, and many others. She has been nominated twice for a Pushcart Prize, and she teaches English at CUNY. *The Transparent Dinner*, her book of poems, was published by Mayapple Press in 2006 and her second book, *Saints & Cannibals*, is due out this fall. Christine was a runner-up to the Poet Laureate of Queens.

Reginald Harris is Systems Department Help Desk and Training Manager for the Pratt Library in Baltimore. Finalist for a Lambda Literary Award for *10 Tongues: Poems* (Three Conditions Press, 2001), he is currently pretending to work on two manuscripts; *12 Rounds: Of Boxers and Other Fighters* and *Autogeography*.

J. M. R. Harrison lives in West Virginia. While she has a doctorate from the University of Virginia in an unrelated field, she now pursues her lifelong interest in poetry at the Writer's Center in Bethesda, MD. Her poems have been published in *Antietam Review, Penwood Review, The Sow's Ear*, and the anthology *Wild Sweet Notes II: More Great Poetry From West Virginia*.

Clarinda Harriss teaches poetry, poetic forms, and editing at Towson University, where she chaired the English Department for a decade and continues to advise *Grub Street*, the university's nationally acclaimed student literary magazine. She has worked for many years with writers in prisons.

Catherine Hartlove holds her M.S. in Professional Writing from Towson University. She teaches writing at two Maryland universities. Recently, she sold a piece of short fiction entitled, "This Side of the Veil," to an anthology.

Bernard Henrie is now a currency day trader living on the edge of the Mojave Desert. He administered social service programs in Los Angeles County for 20 years before becoming a staff writer for an environmental publication in southern California. His publication credits include *MiPOesias, Shampoo*, and *Quarterly Literary Review Singapore*. Four of his poems were anthologized in *The Wild Poetry Anthology* and *The Pirated Poetry Anthology* published by Farfalla Press. Mark Dotty selected his poem as second best for the year in the Interboard Poetry Competition (IBPC) for 2007.

Ahmede Hussain was born in 1978 and has joined Bangladesh's the Daily Star in 2002. His latest work, "Blues for Allah," a novella, has been published in *Colloquy, text theory, critique*, the journal of Monash University, Australia. He has edited 'Brown Writing', an anthology of South Asian fiction in English, which is awaiting publication. Presently he is at work on his first novel. He lives and works in Dhaka.

Karen Karlitz's work has appeared in the *Los Angeles Times, Foliate Oak, Miranda Literary Journal, Long Story Short, Miami Herald, Beverly Hills 90210, Brentwood News*, and the anthology, *Freckles to Wrinkles*, among others. One of her stories was a *Third Glass Woman Prize* finalist, and another chosen for inclusion in the 2007-2008 edition of *The Best of the Foliate Oak*. Additional stories are scheduled to appear in future issues of *Clever Magazine* and *The Stray Branch*. "Marriage, Interrupted" is an excerpt from her novel, "Home Fires," which is now being submitted for publication. She is also at work on a short fiction collection.

Guy Kettelhack has authored, co-authored or contributed to more than 30 non-fiction books. His poetry has appeared in over 25 print and online journals, including *Van Gogh's Ear, Melic Review, New Pleiades, Malleable Jangle, WORM 33, Das Alchymist Poetry Review, the PK list, The Rose & Thorn, Heretics & Half-Lives, Desert Moon Review, Hiss Quarterly, Juked, Anon, Umbrella Journal, Mississippi Crow* and *The Chimaera*. He lives in NYC.

Larry Kimmel is primarily known as a tanka-poet and writer of haibun, though over the years he has been quietly writing longer poems in free verse form. He has appeared in *The Christian Science Monitor* and is a frequent contributor to *Lynx*; *Ribbons*; *red lights*; *gusts*; *Eucalypt*; *bottle rockets*; and other haiku and tanka magazines, both domestically and internationally. His latest books of poetry are *this hunger, tissue-thin* and *Blue Night & the inadequacy of long-stemmed roses* (Modern English Tanka Press). He lives with his wife in the hills of western Massachusetts.

Stephanie King received her MFA in Writing and Literature from Bennington College, where she was the Editor of the *Bennington Review*. Her novella "Ghost Bite" was the winner of the 2006 *Quarterly West* Novella Prize. She is the Assistant Fiction Editor at *Drunken Boat*.

Lidia Kosk is the author of eight books of poems and short stories. In Poland, where she resides, her poems have been published in journals and anthologies, and broadcast in a weekly program of Polish Radio. In the USA, English translations of her poems by Danuta E. Kosk-Kosicka have appeared in several publications, including *International Poetry Review, Passager, Loch Raven Review, September Eleven: Maryland Voices Anthology*, and *Contemporary Writers of Poland*. Most recently her works were featured in the international issue of *The Fourth River and in Against Agamemnon: War Poetry 2009*, edited by James Adams. Her first bilingual book of poems, *niedosyt/ reshapings*, was published in 2003; the second, *Słodka woda, słona woda/ Sweet Water, Salt Water*, in 2009. She is a lawyer, humanitarian, and world traveler. Her most recent visit to the USA was in 2003, when she introduced her first bilingual book to American audiences.

Danuta E. Kosk-Kosicka writes and translates poems in English and Polish. She is the author of two poetry chapbooks, *Between Here and There* and *On the Verge of Light and Shadow*, and translator for the bilingual book of poems by Lidia Kosk, *niedosyt/reshapings*. Her poems have been published in literary journals, anthologies, and magazines in both the U.S. and Poland. She pursues painting and photography; her work has been featured in several shows in both countries. Born in Poland, she holds a Ph.D. in biochemistry from the Polish Academy of Sciences. She has resided in Baltimore, Maryland, since 1981.

David W. Landrum teaches Literature at Grand Valley State University in Allendale, Michigan. His fiction and poetry has appeared in numerous journals, and he edits the on-line poetry journal, *Lucid Rhythms*.

Chuck Levenstein, Ph.D., MSc, is an economist and policy analyst— and poet and writer. He is Professor Emeritus in Department of Work Environment, retiring from teaching in 2003. He is adjunct professor of occupational health at Tufts University School of Medicine and one of the leading researchers concerned with social factors in occupational and environmental health. Dr Levenstein chairs the advisory committee for United SteelWorkers Federally-funded projects and for The New England Consortium. His most recent book (with Greg deLaurier and Mary Lee Dunn), *THE COTTON DUST PAPERS* (2002), concerns the 50-year struggle for recognition of byssinosis ("brown lung") in the U.S. Dr. Levenstein served on the IOM/NAS Committee on Health and Safety Needs of Older Workers. He is Editor Emeritus of *New Solutions*, a quarterly peer-reviewed journal of occupational and environmental health policy and is co-editor of the Baywood series on Work, Health and Environment. Prof. Levenstein is a recipient of the American Public Health Association's award for lifetime contribution to occupational health. He has published widely in poetry e-zines and has appeared previously in *Loch Raven Review*. His three books of poetry are *Lost Baggage, Poems of World War III*, and *Animal, Vegetable*.

Nulty Lynch is a husband, father, poet and fly-fisherman. Not usually all at once, or in that order. He lives in Laurel, Maryland with his wife, two daughters and two dogs. He works for a financial research bureau in Washington D.C. and spends his train commute writing & staring out the window. He has most recently been published in *Shoots and Vines* and *Modern English Tanka*, and will be published in an upcoming issues of *The Stray Branch* and *Yellow Mama*.

Henry F. Mazel has written for *The New York Times*, has a published a novel to his credit, *Murderously Incorrect*, as well as having written numerous stories and articles. His play, *Life and Other Games of Chance* was produced on Theatre Row in New York City. His short film *Nouvelle Vague Repas* is included in the Donnell Library Permanent Collection. He is a member of the Writers Guild of America and The Mystery Writers of America. His latest short story, *Breakfast With Nattie*, will appear in the Fall issue of *Green Silk Journal*.

Dan Maguire's poetry has won local and national awards. He has read at the Library of Congress and led workshops for the National Federation of State Poetry Societies and the Philadelphia Writers Conference. His latest publication is *Finding the Words* from Plan B Press.

Michael Monroe is a poet who has been writing and reading in the Baltimore area for about 15 years. In college, he was the poetry editor for *Grub Street*, Towson University's literary magazine, and since then, he's had poems published in *Manorborn, Loch Raven Review*, and *Poet's Ink*. He's been a member of the Zelda's Inferno writing group and workshop since 2000 and he often does poetry readings with *Gimme Shelter Productions* to raise money and awareness for the homeless in Baltimore.

Yvette Neisser Moreno is a poet and translator whose work has appeared in numerous magazines and anthologies, including *The International Poetry Review, The Potomac Review, Tar River Poetry*, and *Virginia Quarterly Review*. Her translation (from Spanish) of Argentinean Luis Alberto Ambroggio's *Difficult Beauty: Selected Poems* was published by Cross-Cultural Communications in 2009. In addition to working as a professional writer/editor, Moreno teaches poetry and translation at the Writer's Center and has taught poetry in public schools in Maryland, Virginia, and Washington, D.C.

Mark A. Murphy has published poems in *Poetry New Zealand, Poetry Scotland, The Warwick Review* (UK), *The Paris Atlantic Journal* (France), *Poetry Salzburg Review* (Austria), *Istanbul Literature Review* (Turkey), *Del Sol Review* (US), *Tampa Review* (US) and *The Stinging Fly* (Eire).

James B. Nicola has had over ninety poems appear in a score of publications including *The Lyric, Nimrod, Upstart Crow, Mobius*, and *Cider Press Review*, and received the Dana Literary Award for poetry. A stage director by profession, his book *Playing the Audience* won a CHOICE Award as one of the best books of the year.

Amanda K. Norris is a freelance writer and former newspaper reporter. In 2004, she obtained a B.A. from Temple University in Philadelphia, PA. Her articles have been published in *Philadelphia Weekly, Philadephia Style* and *The Weekly Press*. She held a staff position at *The (Norwalk) Hour* for one year beginning in March 2008. She won the Bryn Mawr College Alexandra Preshka Literary Prize for Sophomores for her short story "The Shoes," and her poem "Death by Crocodile" appeared in the inaugural issue of the online cultural journal, *Eve in Hand*. She currently lives in Branford, Ct.

Constantine Pantazonis, a native Baltimorean, is pursuing a degree in Ancient History and intends to teach in Baltimore upon completion of his studies. Using ancient motifs and contemporary culture, Constantine's poetry focuses on social relations and the human condition.

Michael Pedersen is a 24 year old aspiring poet of Caledonian stock. He has been published in a number of magazines and his first Chapbook— 'Part-Truths' —is due for publication by Koo Press later this year. Over the forthcoming period Michael intends to complete a poetry master and fill the role of teacher over in Cambodia under watch of a writing mentor.

Andrea Potos' full-length collection of poems *Yaya's Cloth* was published by Iris Press, and her chapbook of poems *The Perfect Day* was published by Parallel Press. Her poems have been published widely and are forthcoming in *Women's Review of Books, Nimrod, Spillway, Southern Poetry Review, CALYX Journal, Blue Unicorn, Poetry East* and several other journals and anthologies.

Paula Ray is an emerging writer from Wilmington, North Carolina where she teaches music, gigs about town on her saxophone, composes and writes. Some of her poems have appeared or are forthcoming in: *Word Riot, Mad Swirl*, and *A capella Zoo*.

Oliver Rice has received the Theodore Roethke Prize and twice been nominated for a Pushcart Prize. His poems have appeared widely in journals and anthologies in the United States, as well as in Canada, England, Austria, Turkey, and India. His book of poems, *On Consenting to Be a Man*, has been introduced by Cyberwit, a diversified publishing house in the cultural capital Allahabad, India, and is available on Amazon.

Erik Richardson is a freelance writer and school teacher with a number of published articles, essays, and poems. He was a runner-up for the Gahagan prize in poetry last year, and some of his recent poetry has appeared in *Free Verse, Arbor Vitae*, and *The Centrifugal Eye* (featured poet).

John Riebow was born, raised and educated in Philadelphia, where he attended the W. B. School High School of Agriculture Sciences, majoring in Horticulture. He holds a Bachelor of Science degree in Landscape Architecture from Temple University, is a LEED-Accredited Professional, and serves as Director of Design for a design-build-development general contractor. His work has been placed in *Audience, Ensorcelled* and *Forge Journal*. He has been writing fiction, poetry and radio drama scripts for over twenty years and is currently working on a collection of his short fiction.

Ron Riekki has a Ph.D. in Literature & Creative Writing from Western Michigan University. His novel *U.P.* was its publisher's bestselling novel for 35 weeks.

John Riley is the founder and publisher of Morgan Reynolds Publishing, an independent educational publisher in Greensboro, North Carolina. Before founding Morgan Reynolds, he worked as a freelance writer and teacher. His fiction and poetry have appeared in *Corradi, Aberrations, Hardboiled, The Houston Literary Review, SmokeLong Quarterly* and *Hobble Creek Review*.

Michael Salcman was born in Pilsen, Czechoslovakia in 1946, the son of Holocaust survivors, and came to the United States in 1949. He attended the Combined Program in Liberal Arts and Medical Education at Boston University, receiving both the B.A. and M.D. in 1969, and trained in neurophysiology at the National Institutes of Health in Bethesda and in neurological surgery at Columbia University. Salcman has been writing poetry for almost forty years. His earliest published poems date from 1963 through 1977. After a ten-year hiatus, he began to write again. He spent ten summers at the Sarah Lawrence Writers Seminars studying with Tom Lux, Stephen Dobyns, Heather McHugh, Stuart Dischell, D. Nurske, and Deborah Digges. Tom Lux and Dick Allen have been intimately involved in editing his manuscripts for publication.

Don Schaeffer established Enthalpy Press and has published 5 chap books including "Time Meat" and "The Word Cow and the Pig O' Love." Recent poetry has been published in *The Writers Publishing, Loch Raven Review, Lilly Lit, Burning Effigy Press, Understanding Magazine, Melange, Tryst, Quills*, and others. His first book of poetry, *Almost Full* was published by Owl Oak Press early in the summer of 2006. He holds a Ph.D. in Psychology from City University of New York (1975) and lives in Winnipeg, Manitoba with his wife, Joyce.

Adelaide B. Shaw lives in Millbrook, NY with her husband. She has three children and six grandchildren. Her stories have been published in several literary journals, including *By-Line, The Country and Abroad, Bartleby Snopes, Loch Raven Review, American Literary Review, The Writers' Journal, SN Review, Bewildering Stories* and *Storyteller*. In addition to writing fiction, Adelaide writes haiku and other Japanese poetic forms, such as tanka and haibun and has been published widely. Her award winning collection of haiku, *An Unknown Road*, is available at *Modern English Tanka Press*.

Arthur Seeley is a retired teacher and lecturer who has discovered a love for poetry in his retirement and the purchase of a computer. His poetry embraces many forms and disciplines. He was elected by acclaim as Poet Idol for Yorkshire Water 2007 and achieved second place in the 2004 World Haiku Association's annual competition with a Haibun.

Tom Sheehan's books are *Epic Cures* (an IPPY Award winner) and *Brief Cases, Short Spans*, November 2008 from Press 53; *A Collection of Friends* (with an Aldren nomination) and *From the Quickening*, March 2009 from Pocol Press; three completed manuscripts include a collection of cowboy stories, *Where Cowboys Ride Forever, Out of the Universe Endlessly Calling*, contemporary short stories, and a collection of poetry, *All This Earth and Light*. His work is currently in or coming in *Ocean Magazine, Perigee, Rope and Wire Magazine, Qarrtsiluni, Green Silk Journal, Halfway Down the Stairs, Ad Hoc Monadnock, Hawk & Whippoorwill, Eden Waters Press, Ensorcelled, Canopic Jar, SFWP, Lyrical Ballads, Oddville Press, Lock Raven Review, Indite Circle, Northville Review, Yale Anglers Journal, Ozone Park Journal, Camroc Press, Vermont Literary Review, Word Catalyst, Rosebud*, etc., and in books coming from *Press 53, Home of the Brave, Stories in Uniform* and *Milspeak Anthology*. He has ten Pushcart nominations, Noted Story nominations for 2007 and 2008, the Georges Simenon Award for fiction, and a story in the *Dzanc Best of the Web Anthology for 2009*.

Matt Siegel earned his MFA in fiction from Georgia College & State University and currently teaches at Southern Connecticut State University. His works of fiction, nonfiction, and poetry have appeared in *Pebble Lake Review, Redivider* (twice), *So to Speak, Press 53, Pearl, Buffalo Carp*, and elsewhere.

Janice D. Soderling has published translations of poems by several Swedish and Finno-Swedish poets. Her own poetry, fiction, nonfiction and essays appear in many print and online journals based in nine countries. Her fiction and poetry appears in both Swedish and English anthologies. In 2007, she received a cash award as recognition of her past writing in Swedish; in 2009, her poetry was nominated for *Dzanc Best of the Web, Sundance Best of the Net*, and *Pushcart*. She lives in a small Swedish village.

KH Solomon is a retired agricultural engineer, whose career specialized in water management. His poems have appeared or are forthcoming in *ZYZZYVA, English Journal, River Oak Review, Conclave*, and elsewhere.

Shawn Nacona Stroud's poetry has appeared in the *Crescent Moon Journal, Mississippi Crow Magazine, Loch Raven Review, The Poetry Worm*, and *Here and Now*. His work has also appeared in the poetry anthologies *Poetry Pages Volume IV* and *Poetry From The Darkside Volume 2* and was recently nominated for a Pushcart Prize for 2008.

S. Thomas Summers is a teacher of literature and writing at Wayne Hills High School in Wayne, NJ and Passaic County Community College in Wanaque, NJ. He is the author of two chapbooks: *Death Settled Well* (Shadows Ink Publications, 2006) and *Rather, It Should Shine* (Pudding House Press, 2007). His work has appeared in *Umbrella, Triggerfish, Pedestal Magazine, The Oak Bend Review* and other print and electronic journals. His poem "A Fall from Grace" was recently awarded the IBPC poem of the year.

Yermiyahu Ahron Taub is the author of two volumes of poetry *The Insatiable Psalm* (Hershey, Pa.: Wind River Press, 2005) and *What Stillness Illuminated/Vos shtilkayt hot baloykhtn* (West Lafayette, Ind.: Parlor Press, 2008; Free Verse Editions series).

Ray Templeton is a Scottish writer and musician, living in England. His poetry, short fiction and writings on music have appeared widely on the web and in print, and sometimes even other people sing his songs.

Christopher Woods is the author of a prose collection, *Under a Riverbed Sky*, and a collection of stage monologues for actors, *Heart Speak*. His play, *Moonbirds*, about doomed census takers at work in an uninhabited desert country, received its New York City premiere at Personal Space Theatrics. He lives in Houston and in Chappell Hill, Texas.

Stephen Jarrell Williams loves to write, listen to his music, and dance late into the night. He was born in Fort Belvoir, Virginia. His parents are native Texans. He has lived most of his life in California. His poetry has appeared in *Anthology, Avocet, Blue Collar Review, The Broome Review, Byline Magazine, Chronogram Magazine, Fissure Magazine, Freefall, Haight Ashbury Literary Journal, Hawaii Review, HUNGUR, Liquid Imagination, Nerve Cowboy, Mirror Dance, POEM, Poesia, Posey, Purpose, REAL, Tales from the Moonlit Path*, and many others.

Michael T. Young has published two collections of poetry: *Because the Wind Has Question* and *Transcriptions of Daylight*. He received a 2007 Fellowship from the New Jersey State Council on the Arts and received a 2008 William Stafford Award. He has been twice nominated for a Pushcart Prize and received the Chaffin Poetry Award for 2005. His work has appeared or is forthcoming in *Heliotrope, RATTLE, The Same, The Sow's Ear Poetry Review* and many other journals. His work is also in the anthologies *Phoenix Rising* and *Chance of a Ghost*. he currently lives with his wife and two children in Jersey City, New Jersey.

Thane Zander is a retired Navy man and a Bipolar Sufferer. He has used poetry as a means to monitor his illness and life. Part of the recovery was to join online Poetry Forums, one of which has seen him become Director of Challenges and Workshop forums at *Blueline*. He also runs a New Zealand Poets only website, workshops his poems at *Salty Dreams*, and fills the pages at *Babilu Forums*. Thane has had poetry published in *Here and Now, Loch Raven Review, Windjammer Press, Blackmail Press* (volumes 10, 15, 18, 22) and an anthology called *A Bouquet of Poetry*. He has recently completed studies at University for Creative Writing (where *The Free Spirit* scored an A-) and The Music of Pink Floyd. 2009 will find him studying five English papers, working towards a degree in English as well as continuing online poetry. He has a 3/4 finished novel (*Tuwhenga*) on the table.

Fredrick Zydek, before retiring, taught creative writing and theology for many years, first at UNO and later at the College of Saint Mary. He bought a small farm that has a creek running through it, and these days raises soybeans and corn and can go fishing any day of the week he wants— in season. He has published eight collections of poetry.